Recipes
American Cooking: Southern Style

Contents

Foods of the World

D1096819

TIME-LIFE BOOKS, NEW YORK

© 1971 Time Inc. All rights reserved. Published simultaneously in Canada.

Introductory Notes

Techniques for Home Canning

To ensure consistent results in home canning, use standard canning jars or jelly glasses with matching lids. Examine each jar or glass carefully and discard those with covers that do not fit securely and those with cracked or chipped edges. An airtight seal is essential to prevent the spoilage of food.

Wash the jars, glasses, lids and rings in hot soapy water and rinse them in scalding water. Place them in a large deep pot and pour in enough hot water to cover them completely. Bring to a boil over high heat, then turn off the heat while you finish cooking the food that you plan to can. The jars or glasses must be hot when they are filled. (If you have a dishwasher with a sanitizing cycle, simply run the jars, glasses, lids and rings through the cycle, using your usual dishwashing powder, and leave them in the closed machine until you are ready to can.)

To prepare for sealing the glasses, grate a 4-ounce bar of paraffin into the top of a double boiler (preferably one with a pouring spout), and melt the paraffin over hot water.

When the food is ready for canning, lift the jars or glasses from the pot or dishwasher with tongs and stand them upright on a level surface. Leave the lids and rings in the pot (or dishwasher) until you are ready to use them. Fill and seal the jars one at a time, filling each jar to within ⅛ inch of the top or each glass to within ½ inch of the top. Each jar should be sealed quickly and tightly with its ring and lid. (If there is not enough food to fill the last jar or glass completely, do not attempt to seal it. Refrigerate and use within the next week.)

The jelly glasses also should be sealed at once. Pour a single thin layer of hot paraffin over the surface of the jelly, making sure it covers the jelly completely and touches all sides of the glass. If air bubbles appear on the paraffin, prick them immediately with the tip of a knife. Let the glasses rest until the paraffin cools and hardens, then cover with metal lids.

If a recipe calls for finishing the preserving process with a water bath, place the filled and sealed jars side by side on a rack in a canner or other deep large pot. Pour in enough hot (not boiling) water to cover the jars by at least 1 inch, securely cover the pot with its lid, and bring to a boil over moderate heat. Boil for the time recommended in the particular recipe. Then, with tongs, remove the jars from the pot and let them cool at room temperature for about 12 hours. Test the seal by pressing the center of each lid with your forefinger. If the inner lid remains in place, unscrew the outer ring, leaving the seal intact. Store the jar upright in a cool, dry, dark spot. If the lid moves at all, the jar is not properly sealed; in that event, refrigerate and serve the food within the week.

For additional information on canning, see "How to Make Jellies, Jams and Preserves at Home," USDA Home and Garden Bulletin No. 56, and "Making Pickles and Relishes at Home," USDA Home and Garden Bulletin No. 92. These bulletins cost 15 cents each and can be ordered from the Superintendent of Documents, U.S. Government Printing Office, Washington, D.C. 20402.

Extra Mileage for Lard and Oil

After it has been used for deep frying, lard or vegetable oil may be cooled and strained through a fine sieve lined with a double thickness of dampened cheesecloth, then refrigerated in a tightly covered, labeled can or jar. Preserved in this fashion, the fat may be stored for several weeks and re-used two or three times.

How to Handle Chilies

Hot peppers, or chilies, require special handling. Their volatile oils may make both your skin and your eyes burn. While working with chilies wear rubber gloves if you can, and be careful not to touch your face or eyes. After handling the chilies, wash your hands thoroughly with soap and warm water.

To prepare chilies, rinse them clean and pull out the stems under cold running water. Break or cut the pods in half, and brush out the seeds with your fingers. In most cases the ribs inside the pods are thin and may be left intact, but if they seem fleshy, cut them out with a small sharp knife. The chilies may be used at once or soaked in cold salted water for an hour or so to make them less hot.

HORS D'OEUVRE

Benne-Seed Cocktail Biscuits

To make about 8 dozen 1½-inch
   biscuits

½ cup benne seeds (sesame seeds)
2 cups flour
1 teaspoon double-acting baking
   powder
½ teaspoon salt
8 tablespoons butter, chilled and cut
   into ¼-inch bits
4 tablespoons milk
Coarse (kosher) salt

Preheat the oven to 350°. Spread the benne seeds evenly in a shallow baking dish and, stirring occasionally, toast them in the middle of the oven until golden brown. Remove from the oven and set the seeds aside.

Combine the flour, baking powder and salt and sift them into a large chilled bowl. Add the butter bits and, with your fingertips, rub the fat and flour together until they resemble flakes of coarse meal. Pour in the milk and mix with your hands or a spoon until the dough is smooth. Then blend in the benne seeds, wrap the dough in wax paper and refrigerate for at least 1 hour before using.

Preheat the oven to 350°. Cut the chilled dough in half and shape each half into a rectangle. Place one half at a time between two sheets of lightly floured wax paper and roll out the dough paper thin. Gently peel off the top sheet of wax paper and, with a biscuit cutter or the rim of a glass, cut the dough into 1½-inch rounds. Using a metal spatula, carefully transfer the rounds to ungreased baking sheets. Gather the scraps into a ball, shape it into a rectangle and roll it out between sheets of wax paper as before; then cut as many more biscuits as you can.

Bake the biscuits in the middle of the oven for 10 to 12 minutes, or until they are a pale golden color. Slide them onto wire racks and at once sprinkle the tops lightly with the coarse salt. Serve the biscuits at room temperature. The benne-seed cocktail biscuits can safely be kept in a tightly covered jar or tin for 2 or 3 weeks. Before serving, warm and crisp them for a few minutes in a low oven (250°).

Beer Cheese

To make about 1½ cups

1½ teaspoons finely chopped
   garlic
1 tablespoon Worcestershire sauce
½ teaspoon Tabasco
½ teaspoon dry mustard
½ teaspoon salt
1 cup beer
4 cups (1 pound) freshly grated
   sharp natural Cheddar cheese

In a deep bowl, crush the garlic to a paste with a pestle or the back of a spoon. Beat in the Worcestershire, Tabasco, mustard and salt. Then, stirring the mixture constantly, pour in the beer in a slow, thin stream. When the ingredients are well blended, beat in the cheese, a cupful at a time, and continue to beat until the mixture is smooth.

Pack the beer cheese tightly into a 2-cup mold or an earthenware crock. Cover with a lid or foil and refrigerate for at least 24 hours before serving. Beer cheese is traditionally served with crisp crackers as a first course or as an accompaniment to drinks.

Salted Pecans

To make 4 cups

1½ pounds (4 cups) unsalted
   shelled pecans
6 tablespoons unsalted butter,
   melted and cooled
1 tablespoon salt

Preheat the oven to 350°. Place the nuts in a large mixing bowl and pour the butter over them. Toss with a wooden spoon until all the nuts glisten, then toss them with the salt. Transfer the nuts to a shallow roasting pan and spread them out in one layer.

Roast the nuts uncovered for 15 to 20 minutes, tossing them from time to time with a wooden spoon. When the nuts are crisp and golden brown, transfer them to paper towels to drain. Cool to room temperature and serve the pecans at once, or store them in airtight jars in a cool place.

Pickled Shrimp

To make about 2 quarts

2 pounds medium-sized raw shrimp
    (about 21 to 25 to the pound)
1 large onion, peeled, cut crosswise
    into ¼-inch-thick slices and
    separated into rings
2 lemons, cut crosswise into ⅛-
    inch-thick slices
A 1-inch piece of fresh ginger root,
    scraped and cut into paper-thin
    slices

¼ cup finely chopped fresh parsley
4 small bay leaves
2 cups cider vinegar
2 tablespoons mixed pickling spice
½ teaspoon dry mustard
¼ teaspoon ground mace
2 teaspoons salt
½ cup olive oil, combined with
    ½ cup vegetable oil

Shell the shrimp. Devein them by making a shallow incision down their backs with a small sharp knife and lifting out the black or white intestinal vein with the point of the knife. Drop the shrimp into enough lightly salted boiling water to immerse them completely and boil briskly, uncovered for about 3 minutes, or until they are firm and pink. Drain the shrimp, spread them on paper towels and pat them completely dry with fresh paper towels.

Place the shrimp in a deep bowl, add the onion rings, lemon slices, ginger root and parsley, and toss them together gently but thoroughly. Transfer the mixture to two wide-mouthed quart jars, dividing it evenly between them. Tuck 2 bay leaves down the sides of each jar.

Combine the vinegar, pickling spice, mustard, mace and salt in a 1- to 1½-quart enameled or stainless-steel saucepan and bring to a boil over high heat, stirring until the mustard and salt dissolve completely. At once pour the hot spiced liquid over the shrimp mixture by the tablespoonful. Allow each spoonful of liquid to flow completely through to the bottom of the jars before adding more.

To make the jars of pickled shrimp airtight, place a tablespoon upside down in the top of each jar and very slowly pour the olive-and-vegetable-oil mixture over the back of the spoon, letting it trickle off onto the top of the shrimp. Cover the jars with their lids and chill the shrimp for at least 24 hours before serving. (Tightly covered and refrigerated, the shrimp can safely be kept for about 1 month.)

BREAKFAST DISHES

Shrimp Paste

To make about 3 cups

1½ pounds raw shrimp, shelled
 and deveined (see shrimp pilau,
 page 29)
8 tablespoons unsalted butter,
 softened
2 tablespoons pale dry sherry
4 teaspoons strained fresh lemon
 juice

4 teaspoons finely grated onion
½ teaspoon ground mace
½ teaspoon dry mustard
½ teaspoon ground hot red pepper
 (cayenne)
2 teaspoons salt
½ teaspoon ground white pepper

Drop the shrimp into enough boiling water to immerse them completely
and boil briskly, uncovered, for 3 minutes, or until they are firm and
pink. Drain the shrimp, spread them on paper towels and pat them completely dry with fresh towels. Then put the shrimp through the finest
blade of a food grinder. If you lack a food grinder, chop the shrimp as
fine as possible and pound them to a smooth paste with a mortar and pestle or in a bowl with the back of a spoon.

In a deep bowl, cream the butter by beating and mashing it against the
sides of the bowl with the back of a wooden spoon until it is light and
fluffy. Beat in the sherry, lemon juice, onion, mace, mustard, red pepper,
salt and white pepper. When thoroughly incorporated, add the shrimp
and continue to beat until the mixture is smooth. Taste for seasoning.

Transfer the shrimp paste to a 3-cup serving bowl or mold, spreading
it and smoothing the top with a spatula. Cover with foil or plastic wrap
and refrigerate for at least 4 hours, or until the paste is firm to the touch.

Serve the paste directly from the bowl, or unmold it in the following
fashion: Run a thin-bladed knife around the edges of the mold to loosen
it and dip the bottom in hot water. Place an inverted serving plate over
the bowl and, grasping plate and bowl together firmly, turn them over.
Rap the plate on a table and the shrimp paste should slide out easily.

In Charleston, shrimp paste is traditionally served for breakfast, or
with wafers or crackers as an accompaniment for drinks.

Country-Style Sausage with Fried Apple Rings

To serve 6 to 8

2 pounds lean boneless pork, coarsely ground
¼ pound fresh pork fat, finely chopped
1 tablespoon crumbled dried sage leaves
1 teaspoon ground nutmeg, preferably freshly grated
¼ teaspoon ground hot red pepper (cayenne)

1 tablespoon salt
1 teaspoon freshly ground black pepper
3 large firm tart cooking apples, cored but not peeled, cut crosswise into ½-inch-thick rings
Cinnamon sugar made from ¼ cup sugar combined with 2 teaspoons ground cinnamon

Combine the ground pork, pork fat, sage, nutmeg, red pepper, salt and black pepper in a deep bowl and knead vigorously with both hands until the sausage mixture is smooth. On a firm, flat surface, pat and roll the mixture into a thick cylinder about 8 inches long and 3 inches in diameter. Wrap tightly in wax paper or foil and refrigerate for at least 2 hours, or until the sausage is firm. (Covered and refrigerated, the sausage can safely be kept for 3 or 4 days.)

Preheat the oven to its lowest setting. Then line a large shallow baking dish with paper towels and place it in the center of the oven.

Slice the sausage cylinder crosswise into ½-inch-thick round cakes. Place 5 or 6 cakes in an ungreased heavy 10- to 12-inch skillet and set it over moderate heat. Turning the cakes frequently with a slotted spatula, fry them for about 10 minutes, or until they are richly browned on both sides and no trace of pink shows when a cake is pierced with the point of a small sharp knife. As the fat accumulates, draw it off with a bulb baster and reserve in a heatproof bowl.

Transfer the fried cakes to the lined baking dish and keep them warm in the oven. Place 5 or 6 more cakes in the skillet and repeat the entire procedure until all the sausage is fried.

Return enough of the reserved fat to the skillet to come about ½ inch up the sides. Drop half of the apple rings into the hot fat, cover the pan tightly and cook over moderate heat for 2 minutes. Turn the apple rings over with the slotted spatula and sprinkle them evenly with 1 tablespoon of the cinnamon sugar. Then cover the skillet again and cook for 2 minutes longer, or until the apples are tender. Turn the rings over, sprinkle them with 1 tablespoon of cinnamon sugar and drain them on paper towels. Place the rest of the apple rings in the skillet and fry them as before.

Mound the sausage cakes attractively in the center of a large heated platter and arrange the apple rings around them. Serve at once.

Scrambled Brains

To serve 4 to 6

1 pound calf's brains
Distilled white vinegar
1½ teaspoons salt
6 eggs
1 teaspoon Worcestershire sauce
¼ teaspoon Tabasco
Freshly ground black pepper
4 slices bacon
2 tablespoons butter
¼ cup finely chopped onions

Soak the brains in several changes of cold water for 2 hours; then soak them for another hour in acidulated cold water, using 1 tablespoon of distilled white vinegar for every quart of water. Gently pull off as much of the outside membrane as possible without tearing the brains and cut away the white opaque bits at the base.

Place the brains in an enameled saucepan, add 1 tablespoon of vinegar and 1 teaspoon of the salt, and pour in enough water to cover the brains by at least 2 inches. Bring to a boil over high heat, immediately reduce the heat to low and simmer uncovered for 15 to 20 minutes. Drain the brains, spread them on paper towels and pat them completely dry with fresh towels. Cut the brains into ½-inch pieces.

Break the eggs into a bowl, beat them lightly with a table fork, and stir in the Worcestershire, Tabasco, the remaining ½ teaspoon of salt and a few grindings of pepper. Set aside.

In a heavy 10- to 12-inch skillet, fry the bacon over moderate heat, turning the slices with tongs until they are crisp and brown and have rendered all their fat. Transfer the bacon slices to paper towels to drain, then crumble them into bits and set aside.

Add the butter to the fat remaining in the skillet and drop in the onions. Stirring frequently with a wooden spoon, cook for about 5 minutes, until they are soft and translucent but not brown. Add the brains and toss them about with the spoon until they glisten with fat. Pour the egg mixture over the brains and, stirring constantly with the flat of the fork, cook until the eggs begin to form soft, creamy curds. Do not overcook.

Mound the scrambled brains on a heated platter, scatter the reserved bacon bits on top and serve at once.

Eggs Derby

To serve 6

1 pair veal sweetbreads (about
   ½ pound)
Distilled white vinegar
3 cups water
1 cup coarsely diced celery
¼ cup finely chopped onions
2½ teaspoons salt
Freshly ground black pepper
6 tablespoons plus 1 cup heavy
   cream
1 tablespoon butter, softened, plus
   4 tablespoons butter
6 hard-cooked eggs
3 ounces cooked ham, preferably
   country ham, finely ground or

very finely chopped (about ⅓
   cup)
1 teaspoon dry mustard
¼ teaspoon ground white pepper
½ pound firm fresh mushrooms,
   trimmed, wiped with a dampened
   cloth and cut into ½-inch pieces
   including the stems
4 tablespoons flour
3 tablespoons pale dry sherry
¼ cup freshly grated imported
   Parmesan cheese combined with
   ¼ cup freshly grated sharp
   natural Cheddar cheese
½ cup slivered blanched almonds

Soak the sweetbreads for 2 hours in enough cold water to cover them by at least 1 inch, changing the water every 30 minutes or so; then soak them for another hour in acidulated cold water, using 1 tablespoon of white vinegar for each quart of water. Gently pull off as much of the outside membrane as possible without tearing the sweetbreads, and cut the two lobes from the tube between them with a small sharp knife; discard the tube.

Place the sweetbreads in a small enameled saucepan and add 3 cups of water, the celery, onions, 1 teaspoon of salt and a few grindings of black pepper. Bring to a boil over high heat, then reduce the heat to its lowest point and simmer uncovered for 15 to 20 minutes. Drain, cut the sweetbreads into ¼-inch bits and drop them into a bowl with 1 cup of the cream. Strain the cooking liquid through a fine sieve and reserve 1 cup.

Meanwhile, preheat the oven to 350°. With a pastry brush, spread the tablespoon of softened butter evenly over the bottom and sides of an 8- or 9-inch baking-serving dish about 2 to 3 inches deep.

Peel the hard-cooked eggs and cut them lengthwise in half. Set the egg whites aside. Drop the yolks into a small bowl and, with the back of a fork, mash them to a smooth purée. Stir in the ground ham, mustard, ½ teaspoon of salt, ⅛ teaspoon of the white pepper and the remaining 6 tablespoons of cream. Taste for seasoning. Spoon the egg-yolk mixture into the egg-white halves, dividing it evenly among them and mounding the stuffing slightly. Arrange the eggs in one layer in the buttered baking dish and set aside.

In a heavy 10- to 12-inch skillet, melt the 4 tablespoons of butter over moderate heat. When the foam begins to subside, add the mushrooms and, stirring frequently, cook for 8 to 10 minutes, or until the liquid that accumulates in the pan has evaporated completely. Do not let the mushrooms brown. Stir in the flour and, when it is completely absorbed, pour in the remaining cup of cream and the reserved cup of sweetbread cooking liquid. Stirring the mixture constantly with a whisk, bring to a boil, reduce the heat to low, and simmer for 3 or 4 minutes to remove any taste of raw flour. Then stir in the sweetbreads, sherry, the remaining teaspoon of salt and ⅛ teaspoon of white pepper. Taste for seasoning.

Ladle the sweetbreads-and-mushroom mixture over the stuffed eggs and sprinkle with the cheese and almonds. Bake in the upper third of the oven for 20 to 25 minutes, or until the sauce bubbles and the cheese is delicately browned. Serve at once directly from the baking dish.

Kentucky Scramble

To serve 4

6 slices lean bacon
1 tablespoon butter
1 cup fresh corn kernels, cut from 3
    medium-sized ears of corn, or
    substitute 1 cup canned or
    defrosted frozen corn kernels,
thoroughly drained
½ cup finely chopped green pepper
¼ cup finely chopped pimiento
1½ teaspoons salt
⅛ teaspoon freshly ground black
    pepper
6 eggs

In a heavy 10- to 12-inch ungreased skillet, fry the bacon over moderate heat. Turn the slices with tongs until they are crisp and brown, then transfer them to paper towels to drain.

Pour off all but 3 tablespoons of the fat remaining in the skillet and in its place add the butter. Drop in the corn and stir over moderate heat for 1 or 2 minutes until the kernels glisten. Then add the green pepper, pimiento, salt and black pepper and cook uncovered, stirring frequently, for 5 minutes, or until the vegetables are soft but not brown.

Break the eggs into a bowl, beat them lightly with a table fork, and pour them into the skillet. Stirring with the flat of the fork or a rubber spatula, cook over low heat until the eggs begin to form soft, creamy curds. Mound the eggs on a heated platter, arrange the bacon slices attractively on top and serve at once.

Boiled Grits

To serve 4 to 6

	1 cup regular white hominy grits,
5 cups water	not the quick-cooking variety
1 teaspoon salt	1 tablespoon butter, softened

In a heavy 1½- to 2-quart saucepan, bring the water and salt to a boil over high heat. Pour in the hominy grits slowly enough so that the boiling continues at a rapid rate. Stir constantly with a wooden spoon to keep the mixture smooth.

Reduce the heat to low and, stirring occasionally, simmer the grits tightly covered for 30 minutes. Stir in the butter and mound the grits in a heated bowl. Serve at once with more butter, salt and black pepper to taste.

Fried Grits

To serve 4 to 6

2 tablespoons butter, softened, plus	1 cup regular white hominy grits,
4 to 8 tablespoons butter	not the quick-cooking variety
5 cups plus 2 tablespoons cold water	1 egg
2 teaspoons salt	½ cup flour

With a pastry brush, spread 1 tablespoon of the softened butter over the bottom and sides of a shallow 9-by-13-inch baking dish and set aside.

In a heavy 1½- to 2-quart saucepan, bring 5 cups of water and the salt to a boil over high heat. Pour in the hominy grits slowly enough so that the boiling continues at a rapid rate. Stir constantly with a wooden spoon to keep the mixture smooth.

Reduce the heat to low and, stirring occasionally, simmer the grits tightly covered for 30 minutes. Stir in the remaining tablespoon of softened butter. When it is absorbed, spoon the hot grits into the buttered dish and smooth the top with a metal spatula. Cool to room temperature, cover with plastic wrap or foil, and refrigerate for at least 4 hours, or until the grits are firm to the touch.

Preheat the oven to its lowest setting. Line a large shallow baking dish with paper towels and place it in the middle of the oven.

With a sharp knife, cut the chilled grits into cakes approximately 2 inches square. Beat the egg lightly with the remaining 2 tablespoons of cold water and, one at a time, immerse the cakes in the mixture. Then roll each cake in the flour to coat both sides lightly and evenly.

In a heavy 10- to 12-inch skillet, melt 4 tablespoons of butter over moderate heat. When the foam begins to subside, add 7 or 8 of the hominy-grit cakes and fry them for about 3 minutes on each side, turning them over with a spatula. When the cakes are a golden brown, transfer them to the lined dish to drain and keep them warm in the oven while you fry the rest, 7 or 8 at a time. Add more butter to the skillet as necessary.

Arrange the fried grits attractively on a heated platter and serve them at once, with sorghum or corn or maple syrup.

Hominy Grits Soufflé

To serve 4 to 6

2 cups water	1 tablespoon strained bacon fat, or
1 teaspoon salt	substitute 1 tablespoon lard
½ cup white hominy grits	4 egg yolks, beaten
1 tablespoon butter, softened, plus	Freshly ground black pepper
8 tablespoons (1 quarter-pound	4 egg whites
stick) unsalted butter, cut into bits	¼ cup dry bread crumbs

Preheat the oven to 350°. Pour the water and salt into a heavy 1½- to 2-quart saucepan and bring to a boil over high heat. Slowly pour in the grits, stirring constantly and pouring slowly enough so that the boiling continues at a rapid rate. Stir constantly with a wooden spoon to keep the mixture smooth. Cover the pan tightly, reduce the heat to low and, stirring occasionally, simmer 15 minutes.

Meanwhile, lightly coat the bottom and sides of a 1½- to 2-quart casserole with the tablespoon of softened butter. Set aside.

Remove the saucepan from the heat and with a wooden spoon, beat into the grits the butter bits, bacon fat, egg yolks and several grindings of black pepper.

In a large mixing bowl, beat the egg whites with a whisk or a rotary or electric beater until they are stiff enough to form firm, unwavering peaks on the beater when it is lifted from the bowl. With a rubber spatula, fold the egg whites into the hominy grits mixture, then pour it into the casserole, smoothing the top with the spatula. Sprinkle evenly with the bread crumbs and bake in the middle of the oven for 45 minutes, until the soufflé has puffed and the top is golden brown. Serve at once, directly from the casserole.

Turkey Hash

To serve 6

4 tablespoons butter
2 tablespoons vegetable oil
1½ cups finely chopped onions
¼ cup finely chopped green pepper
½ pound firm fresh mushrooms, trimmed, wiped with a dampened cloth and cut lengthwise, including the stems, into ⅛-inch-thick slices

¼ cup flour
2 cups fresh turkey stock (page 47), or fresh or canned chicken stock
4 cups finely diced roasted turkey (page 46)
¼ cup finely chopped fresh parsley
1 tablespoon Worcestershire sauce
1 teaspoon salt
½ cup heavy cream, if necessary

In a heavy 12-inch skillet, melt the butter in the oil over moderate heat. When the foam begins to subside, add the onions and green pepper and, stirring frequently, cook for about 5 minutes, until they are soft but not brown. Add the mushrooms and, stirring occasionally, cook for 8 to 10 minutes, or until almost all the liquid that accumulates in the pan has evaporated. Do not let the mushrooms brown.

Mix in the flour and, when it is completely absorbed, pour in the stock. Stir with a whisk until the sauce comes to a boil, thickens lightly and is smooth. Reduce the heat to low, add the turkey, parsley, Worcestershire and salt and, stirring frequently with a spoon, simmer for 3 or 4 minutes to heat the hash through. If the hash is too dry for your taste, stir in up to ½ cup heavy cream by the tablespoonful.

Transfer the hash to a heated platter and serve it at once, accompanied, if you like, by batty cakes (below).

Lacy-edged Batty Cakes

These are the cornmeal batter cakes that always accompany turkey hash at a traditional Kentucky Derby breakfast.

To make about 2 dozen

¾ cup white cornmeal, preferably water-ground
½ teaspoon double-acting baking powder
½ teaspoon baking soda

½ teaspoon salt
1 cup buttermilk
1 egg, lightly beaten
½ cup bacon fat, or substitute ¼ pound butter, softened

If you are using regular-ground cornmeal, combine it with the baking powder, soda and salt, and sift them together into a bowl. If you are using water-ground cornmeal, pour it into a bowl and stir in the baking powder, soda and salt. Pour in the buttermilk and beat vigorously with a spoon until it is completely absorbed. Then add the egg and continue to beat until the batter is smooth.

Heat a heavy griddle over high heat until a drop of water flicked onto it steams for a second and evaporates. With a pastry brush, grease the griddle lightly with the bacon fat or butter.

Pour about 1 tablespoon of batter onto the griddle for each batty cake. Fry 4 at a time for 2 to 3 minutes, until the cakes begin to bubble and the bottoms brown. Then turn them over with a spatula and brown the other side. Stack the finished cakes on a heated plate and drape foil over them to keep them warm while you fry the rest. Stir the batter before baking each batch of cakes and brush more bacon fat or butter on the griddle as necessary. Serve the batty cakes as soon as they are all cooked, as an accompaniment to turkey hash or like pancakes with butter and strained honey.

Egg Croquettes

To make 12 croquettes

3 tablespoons butter
1¼ cups flour
1 cup milk
7 hard-cooked eggs, finely chopped
1 small onion, peeled and finely grated
¼ cup finely chopped fresh parsley
1 teaspoon dry mustard

¼ teaspoon ground hot red pepper (cayenne)
1½ teaspoons celery salt
1 cup soft fresh crumbs made from homemade-type white bread, pulverized in a blender or finely shredded with a fork
1 egg
Vegetable oil for deep frying

In a heavy 8- to 10-inch skillet, melt the butter over moderate heat. When the foam begins to subside, mix in ¼ cup of the flour. Then, stirring the mixture constantly with a wire whisk, pour in the milk in a slow, thin stream. Cook over high heat until the sauce comes to a boil, thickens heavily and is smooth. Reduce the heat to low and simmer for about 3 minutes to remove any taste of flour. Remove the skillet from the heat and stir the chopped eggs, grated onion and parsley into the sauce. Add the mustard, red pepper and celery salt, and taste for seasoning.

With a rubber spatula, scrape the contents of the skillet onto a large platter and spread it about ½ inch thick. Cover with plastic wrap and refrigerate for about 3 hours, or until the croquette mixture is firm.

Divide the mixture into 12 equal parts and, with your hands, shape each one into a cylinder about 3 inches long and 1 inch in diameter, or into 2-inch balls or cones. Spread the remaining cup of flour on one plate and the bread crumbs on another. Beat the egg lightly in a shallow bowl. Bread the croquettes one at a time by lightly coating them with the flour,

Continued on next page

immersing them in the egg, then rolling them in the crumbs. Arrange the croquettes side by side on wax paper and refrigerate them for about 20 minutes to firm the coating.

Pour vegetable oil into a deep fryer or large heavy saucepan to a depth of 2 to 3 inches and heat the oil until it reaches a temperature of 350° on a deep-frying thermometer. Deep-fry the croquettes, 3 or 4 at a time, turning them with a slotted spoon for about 4 minutes, or until they are golden brown on all sides. As they brown, transfer the croquettes to paper towels to drain while you deep-fry the rest. Serve at once.

Fried Cheese Grits

To serve 4 to 6

1 tablespoon butter, softened, plus	quick-cooking variety
4 to 8 tablespoons butter	1½ cups (6 ounces) freshly grated
5 cups water	mild natural Cheddar cheese
1 teaspoon salt	1 egg, lightly beaten
1 cup white hominy grits, not the	½ cup flour

With a pastry brush, spread the tablespoon of softened butter over the bottom and sides of a 12-by-8-by-2-inch baking dish and set aside.

In a heavy 1½- to 2-quart saucepan, bring the water and salt to a boil over high heat. Pour in the grits slowly enough so that the boiling continues at a rapid rate, stirring constantly with a wooden spoon to keep the mixture smooth.

Reduce the heat to low and, stirring occasionally, simmer the grits tightly covered for 30 minutes. Stir in the grated cheese and, when it is absorbed, spoon the mixture into the buttered baking dish and smooth the top with a metal spatula. Cool to room temperature, cover with plastic wrap or foil, and refrigerate for at least 4 hours, or until the grits are firm to the touch.

Preheat the oven to its lowest setting. Line a jelly-roll pan with a double thickness of paper towels and place it in the middle of the oven.

With a sharp knife, cut the grits into cakes approximately 2 inches square. One at a time, immerse the cakes in the beaten egg. Then roll each cake in the flour to coat both sides lightly and evenly, placing them side by side on a sheet of wax paper as you proceed.

In a heavy 10- to 12-inch skillet, melt 4 tablespoons of butter over moderate heat. When the foam begins to subside, add 7 or 8 of the cakes and fry them for about 3 minutes on each side, turning them over with a spatula. When the cakes are a golden brown, transfer them to the paper-lined pan to drain and keep them warm in the oven while you fry the remaining cakes similarly. Add butter to the skillet whenever necessary.

Arrange the fried grits on a heated platter and serve them at once.

SOUPS & STEWS

Black Bean Soup

To serve 8

2 quarts water
2 cups (1 pound) dried black beans
3 tablespoons butter
2 cups finely chopped onions
½ cup finely chopped scraped carrots
½ cup finely chopped celery
1½ teaspoons finely chopped garlic
1 to 2 quarts chicken stock, fresh or canned
1½ pounds smoked ham hocks

1 tablespoon distilled white vinegar
1 large bay leaf
1 teaspoon salt
1 tablespoon strained fresh lemon juice
Freshly ground black pepper
½ cup dry Madeira
1 lemon, cut crosswise into ⅛-inch-thick slices
2 hard-cooked eggs, finely chopped
1 tablespoon finely chopped fresh parsley

In a heavy 3- to 4-quart saucepan, bring the water to a boil over high heat. Drop in the beans, cook briskly, uncovered, for 2 minutes, then turn off the heat. Set aside to soak uncovered for about 1 hour.

Meanwhile, melt the butter in a heavy 4- to 5-quart casserole. When the foam begins to subside, add the onions, carrots, celery and garlic. Stirring frequently, cook over moderate heat for about 5 minutes, or until the vegetables are soft but not brown.

Drain the soaked beans through a sieve or colander set over a deep bowl and transfer them to the casserole. Measure the soaking liquid, add enough chicken stock to make 2½ quarts, and pour the mixture into the casserole. Stir in the ham hocks, vinegar, bay leaf and salt, and bring to a boil over high heat. Then reduce the heat to low, cover the casserole partially, and simmer for 2 hours, or until the beans are tender and can be easily mashed against the sides of the pan with a spoon.

Discard the ham hocks and bay leaf. Purée the soup through a food mill or rub it through a fine sieve with the back of a spoon.

Add the lemon juice and a few grindings of pepper, return the soup to the casserole and, stirring constantly, bring it to a simmer over moderate heat. Taste for seasoning and stir in the Madeira.

Ladle the soup into a heated tureen or individual heated soup plates and place the lemon slices on top. Sprinkle with the finely chopped hard-cooked eggs and the chopped parsley and serve at once.

She-Crab Soup

To serve 4

4 quarts water
2 tablespoons plus 1½ teaspoons
  salt
12 live blue she crabs, each about 4
  inches wide and weighing about
  ½ pound
4 tablespoons butter
1 tablespoon flour
2 cups milk

2 cups heavy cream
1½ teaspoons finely grated onions
1 teaspoon finely grated fresh lemon
  peel
½ teaspoon ground mace
½ teaspoon ground white pepper
3 tablespoons pale dry sherry
1 tablespoon finely chopped fresh
  parsley

Bring 4 quarts of water and 2 tablespoons of salt to a boil in an 8- to 10-quart pot. Drop in the crabs and return the water to a boil. Reduce the heat to low, cover tightly and simmer for 15 minutes. Drain the crabs, then clean *(page 32)* and shell them. Set the meat and roe aside.

In a heavy 3- to 4-quart saucepan, melt the butter over moderate heat. When the foam begins to subside, add the flour and mix well. Stirring the mixture constantly with a wire whisk, pour in the milk and cream in a slow thin stream and cook over high heat until the sauce comes to a boil, thickens slightly and is smooth.

Stir in the crabmeat and the crab roe, the onions, lemon peel, mace, the remaining 1½ teaspoons of salt and the white pepper. Reduce the heat to low and simmer partially covered for 20 minutes. Stir in the sherry, taste for seasoning, and pour the soup into a heated tureen or individual soup plates. Sprinkle the top with the parsley and serve the soup at once.

Virginia Peanut Soup

To serve 6 to 8

8 tablespoons (1 quarter-pound
  stick) unsalted butter, cut into
  bits
½ cup finely chopped onions
½ cup finely chopped celery
3 tablespoons flour
2 quarts chicken stock, freshly made
  or canned

2 cups smooth peanut butter, at
  room temperature
¼ teaspoon celery salt
1 teaspoon salt
1 tablespoon strained fresh lemon
  juice
½ cup ground peanuts

In a heavy 3- to 4-quart casserole, melt the butter bits over moderate heat. When the foam subsides, drop in the onions and celery and cook uncovered, stirring frequently, for 5 to 8 minutes, or until the vegetables are soft but have not yet begun to brown. Stir in the flour with a wooden spoon and, when it is thoroughly incorporated, pour in the chicken stock.

Stirring constantly with a whisk, bring to a boil over high heat until the mixture thickens lightly and is smooth. Reduce the heat to low and simmer, partially covered, for 30 minutes, stirring occasionally. Pour the contents of the casserole into a fine sieve set over a bowl, pressing down hard on the vegetables with the back of a spoon before discarding the pulp.

Scrape the peanut butter into a large mixing bowl and whisk in the stock, ¼ cup at a time. After all of the liquid has been added and the soup is smooth, return it to the casserole. Stir in the celery salt, salt and lemon juice, and bring to a simmer over moderate heat. When the soup is hot (do not let it boil), pour it into a heated tureen or individual soup bowls. Present the ground peanuts in a small bowl, to be sprinkled on the soup by each diner.

Conch Chowder

To serve 6 to 8

2½ pounds cooked conch meat, thoroughly defrosted if frozen
½ pound lean salt pork or bacon, finely chopped
2 medium-sized onions, peeled and cut crosswise into ¼-inch-thick slices
1½ teaspoons finely chopped garlic

4 medium-sized firm ripe tomatoes, washed, cored and coarsely chopped
1 large boiling potato, peeled and cut into ½-inch cubes
1 tablespoon uncooked long-grain white rice
3 medium-sized bay leaves
1 quart water
A 13-ounce can evaporated milk

Put the conch meat through the finest blade of a food grinder and set aside in a small bowl.

In a heavy 5- to 6-quart casserole, fry the salt pork or bacon over moderate heat, stirring frequently, until the bits are crisp and brown and have rendered all their fat. Add the sliced onions and chopped garlic and, stirring frequently, cook for about 5 minutes until the onions are soft and translucent but not brown.

Stir in the conch meat, tomatoes, potato, rice, bay leaves and water, and bring to a boil over high heat. Reduce the heat to low and simmer partially covered for 1 hour. Pour in the evaporated milk and stir until the chowder is heated through, but do not allow it to come to a boil.

Taste for seasoning and serve at once from a heated tureen or in individual soup plates.

NOTE: Evaporated milk is a traditional ingredient in conch chowder. Introduced about 1885, evaporated milk required no refrigeration and quickly became a popular product in Florida as well as other Deep-South states. Even today it is widely used in Southern cooking.

Shrimp-and-Oyster Gumbo

To serve 10 to 12

8 tablespoons butter
1 pound fresh okra, thinly sliced,
  or substitute two 10-ounce
  packages of frozen okra,
  thoroughly defrosted and thinly
  sliced
1 cup finely chopped onions
½ cup finely chopped green pepper
1 teaspoon finely chopped garlic
2 tablespoons flour
4 cups chicken stock, fresh or
  canned
6 medium-sized firm ripe tomatoes,
  washed, cored and coarsely
  chopped
6 fresh parsley sprigs and 1 large

bay leaf, tied together with
  kitchen cord
½ teaspoon crumbled dried thyme
2 teaspoons salt
Freshly ground black pepper
1½ pounds small raw shrimp
  (about 30 to the pound)
24 shucked oysters, thoroughly
  defrosted if frozen
2 teaspoons strained fresh lemon
  juice
2 teaspoons Worcestershire sauce
½ teaspoon ground hot red pepper
  (cayenne)
2 cups freshly cooked Southern dry
  rice *(page 72)*

In a heavy 10- to 12-inch skillet, melt 4 tablespoons of the butter over moderate heat. When the foam begins to subside, add the okra. Stirring constantly, cook until the okra stops "roping," that is, until the white threads the vegetable produces disappear. Remove the pan from the heat and set aside.

Over moderate heat, melt the remaining 4 tablespoons of butter in a heavy 3- to 4-quart soup pot or casserole. When the foam subsides, add the onions, green pepper and garlic, and cook for about 5 minutes, or until the vegetables are soft but not brown. Add the flour and cook for 2 or 3 minutes, stirring constantly with a wire whisk. Still whisking, pour in the chicken stock in a slow, thin stream. Then add the okra, the tomatoes, parsley and bay leaf, thyme, salt and a few grindings of black pepper. Bring to a boil, reduce the heat to low, and simmer partially covered for 30 minutes.

Meanwhile, shell the shrimp. Devein them by making a shallow incision down their backs with a small sharp knife and lifting out the black or white intestinal vein with the point of the knife.

Drop the shrimp into the gumbo and simmer for 5 minutes; add the oysters and continue to simmer for 2 or 3 minutes longer, until they plump up and their edges begin to curl. Pick out and discard the parsley and bay leaf, stir the lemon juice, Worcestershire sauce and red pepper into the gumbo and taste for seasoning.

Serve in 10 or 12 heated soup plates, heaping up a small mound of dry rice in the bottom of each plate and ladling the shrimp-and-oyster gumbo over the rice.

Brunswick Stew

To serve 6 to 8

Two 2½- to 3-pound chickens,
each cut into 8 pieces, or
substitute 5 to 6 pounds rabbit,
cut into serving pieces and
thoroughly defrosted if frozen
2 pounds boneless chuck or
shoulder of veal in 1 piece,
trimmed of excess fat
1 teaspoon salt
Freshly ground black pepper
4 tablespoons vegetable oil
2 cups thinly sliced onions
2 cups coarsely chopped celery,
including 2 inches of the green
tops
1 ham bone (about 2 pounds),
preferably from baked Smithfield
or country ham (page 52 or 61),
sawed into 2-inch pieces
(optional)
1 medium-sized bay leaf
1 teaspoon basil

3 sprigs parsley
1 fresh hot red chili, washed, seeded
and crushed (caution: see note,
page 3)
3 pounds (about 9) tomatoes,
peeled, seeded and coarsely
chopped (see shrimp pilau, page
29)
1 pound fresh butter beans or wax
beans (4 cups), washed and
trimmed
8 tablespoons (1 quarter-pound
stick) unsalted butter, cut into
bits
4 cups fresh corn kernels, cut from
about 8 large ears of corn, or
substitute 4 cups thoroughly
defrosted frozen corn kernels
1½ pounds (about 4) medium-
sized boiling potatoes, peeled,
boiled and coarsely mashed
(about 4 cups)
¼ cup finely chopped parsley

Sprinkle the chicken and chuck (or veal) with the salt and several grindings of black pepper. In an 8- to 10-quart casserole, heat the vegetable oil
until very hot but not smoking. Add the chicken a few pieces at a time,
and fry over moderately high heat, turning the pieces frequently, until
golden brown. Transfer the chicken to a platter. In the remaining fat, similarly brown the chuck (or veal) on all sides, then transfer it to the platter of chicken. Pour off all but a thin film of the oil from the casserole,
add the onions and celery and, stirring constantly, cook over moderate
heat until the vegetables are soft but not brown. Return the chicken and
meat to the casserole, and add the ham bone (if you are using it), bay
leaf, basil, parsley sprigs, chili and tomatoes. Pour in enough cold water
to cover the ingredients by 1 inch and bring to a boil over high heat.
Then lower the heat and simmer tightly covered for 35 to 45 minutes, or
until the chicken is tender. With tongs or a slotted spoon, transfer the
chicken to a platter or cutting board, leaving the other meat in the pot.

Cover the casserole again and simmer for about 1 hour longer, or until
the meat shows no resistance when pierced deeply with the prongs of a
large fork. Transfer the meat and ham bone to the platter with the chicken.

Add the beans to the casserole and cook uncovered over high heat for
10 to 15 minutes, or until they are tender but still resistant to the bite.

Continued on next page   21

With a small knife, remove the skin and bones from the chicken and discard them. Cut off any meat from the ham bone if you have used it, and cut the chicken meat and beef or veal into 1-inch pieces. Return all the pieces to the casserole along with any juices that may have accumulated on the platter. Stir in the butter and the corn. Simmer the stew uncovered for 5 minutes, and stir in the mashed potatoes. Stirring frequently, cook for an additional 10 minutes, until the potatoes have been absorbed by the liquid and have thickened the stew. Add the chopped parsley and taste for seasoning.

Serve the stew directly from the casserole, or from a heated bowl. Brunswick stew is often served over Southern dry rice *(Recipe Index)*.

Catfish Stew

To serve 4

5 slices lean bacon	1 pound catfish trimmings: the
1½ cups finely chopped onions	head, tail and bones of the fish
6 medium-sized firm ripe tomatoes,	2 tablespoons Worcestershire sauce
washed, cored and cut into 1½-	½ teaspoon Tabasco
inch pieces	2 teaspoons salt
2 large boiling potatoes, peeled and	Freshly ground black pepper
cut into 1-inch cubes (about 3	2 pounds catfish fillets, cut into
cups)	1½-inch pieces

In a heavy 4- to 6-quart casserole, fry the bacon slices over moderate heat, turning them with tongs until they are crisp and brown and have rendered all their fat. Transfer them to paper towels to drain, then crumble them into small bits and set aside.

Add the onions to the fat remaining in the casserole and, stirring frequently, cook over moderate heat for about 5 minutes, until they are soft and translucent but not brown. Stir in the tomatoes, potatoes, catfish trimmings, Worcestershire, Tabasco, salt and a few grindings of pepper and bring to a boil over high heat. Reduce the heat to low, cover tightly and simmer for 30 minutes.

With tongs or a slotted spoon, remove the catfish trimmings and discard them. Add the catfish fillets and the reserved bacon and mix well. Cover the casserole tightly again and continue to simmer over low heat for 8 to 10 minutes, or until the fish flakes easily when prodded gently with a fork. Taste for seasoning and serve the stew at once, either directly from the casserole or from a large heated bowl.

Terrapin Stew

To serve 4 to 6

6 live terrapin, 5 to 7 inches each, or substitute 2 quarts canned or thoroughly defrosted frozen terrapin meat plus ½ to 1½ cups chicken stock

½ pound unsalted butter, cut into bits
1 teaspoon salt
¼ teaspoon ground hot red pepper (cayenne)
½ cup dry sherry

It takes 3 to 4 hours to prepare terrapin stew with live terrapin, but you may, if you wish, parboil, clean and cook the terrapin, refrigerate them tightly covered, and complete the stew the following day.

At least 1 hour before you are ready to cook the terrapin, place them in a large basin filled with cold water. Let them soak for about an hour, changing the water frequently.

Fill a 10-quart stock pot or casserole three quarters full of cold water and bring to a boil over high heat. Drop in the terrapin, immersing them completely, and boil for 10 minutes. Then drain and transfer the terrapin to a cutting board and let them cool to lukewarm. Pull out the head and feet to expose as much of the meat as possible and, with your fingers or a rough towel, rub off the flaky skin and scales.

Fill the stock pot again with cold water, bring to a boil and drop the terrapin into the pot. When the water returns to a boil, lower the heat and simmer gently, uncovered, for about 1 hour. To test for doneness, lift one of the terrapin up by a hind leg; if it separates from the body, the terrapin are done.

Transfer the terrapin to a large bowl. While you clean them, boil the cooking liquid uncovered over high heat until it has reduced to about 2 cups, and is thick and syrupy.

To clean the terrapin, lift away and discard the top shell of each terrapin one at a time. Adhering to the upper shell or the top of the meat will be thin, leathery-looking lungs and sandbags; cut away and discard them. Then cut off and discard the head, tail and feet. Cut open the meat, remove and set aside the liver, and cut away and discard the gall bladder (being careful not to puncture it). Then pull out the lower intestines, located at the back of the terrapin, and discard them.

Slice the liver as thin as possible and set it aside in a mixing bowl. Pick over the leg and body meat, removing and discarding the bones. Chop the meat as fine as you can.

If there are any eggs in the terrapin, wash them under cold running water, carefully peel off their membranes, and set the eggs aside.

If you are using canned terrapin meat, simply mince it, reserving all

Continued on next page

the canning liquid. Measure the liquid, augment it with enough chicken stock to make 2 cups, and complete the recipe as described below.

When you are ready to serve the terrapin stew, melt 8 tablespoons of the butter bits in a 10- to 12-inch skillet. Stir in the 2 cups of stock, then slowly stir in the remaining butter, salt, cayenne and sherry. Add the chopped terrapin meat and eggs, and simmer for 10 minutes, then transfer the stew to a heated tureen and serve at once, accompanied, if you like, by a cruet of sherry, to be added to the stew by each diner.

Kentucky Burgoo

This distinctive Kentucky stew originally included game—particularly rabbit or squirrel—from the woods of Kentucky, and usually was cooked in vast quantities in an iron kettle over an open fire.

To serve 6 to 8

2 pounds boneless beef shank, trimmed of excess fat
1½ pounds beef bones
½ pound lean boneless lamb, trimmed of excess fat
A 2- to 2½-pound chicken, cut into 6 or 8 pieces
A 1-inch piece fresh hot red chili, seeded *(caution: see note, page 3)*
1 tablespoon salt
Freshly ground black pepper
3 quarts water
2 medium-sized potatoes, peeled and diced (2 cups)
2 cups finely chopped onions
2 cups fresh kernels cut from about 4 large ears of corn, or substitute 2 cups frozen corn kernels, thoroughly defrosted

3 or 4 medium-sized carrots, scraped and cut crosswise into ¼-inch-thick slices (about 2 cups)
6 medium-sized ripe tomatoes, cored and coarsely chopped
¼ pound butter beans or wax beans, washed, trimmed and cut crosswise into halves (about 1 cup)
1 medium-sized green pepper, halved, seeded, deribbed and cut into ½-inch pieces
½ pound fresh okra, washed, trimmed and cut into 1-inch dice (about 1 cup), or substitute frozen okra, thoroughly defrosted and cut into 1-inch dice
1 teaspoon finely chopped garlic
1 cup finely chopped fresh parsley

Combine the beef shank, beef bones, lamb, chicken, chili, salt, a liberal grinding of black pepper and the water in a heavy 6- to 8-quart casserole. Bring to a boil over high heat, meanwhile skimming off the foam and scum as they rise to the surface.

Reduce the heat to low and simmer partially covered for 30 to 40 minutes, or until the chicken is tender. Remove the chicken pieces with tongs or a slotted spoon, and place them on a plate.

Cover the casserole partially again and simmer for about 1½ hours longer, or until the beef and lamb are tender and show no resistance when pierced deeply with the point of a small skewer or sharp knife. Add the beef and lamb to the plate with the chicken. Remove the beef bones and chili and discard them.

Drop the potatoes, onions, corn, carrots, tomatoes, beans, green pepper, okra and garlic into the stock remaining in the casserole. Stirring from time to time, bring to a boil over high heat. Reduce the heat to low and simmer uncovered for 1½ hours. Check the pot from time to time and add up to 2 cups more water, if the stew seems too thick.

With a small knife, remove the skin and bones from the chicken and discard them. Cut the chicken meat, beef shank and lamb into 1-inch pieces and return them to the casserole. Stirring frequently, simmer the burgoo until the meat is heated through. Then stir in the parsley and taste for seasoning.

Serve directly from the casserole or from a heated bowl. Traditionally burgoo is accompanied by cornbread and followed by wedges of pie.

Okra Stew
To serve 6 to 8

½ pound salt pork, with rind removed, cut into ¼-inch-thick slices
8 chicken wings
1 cup coarsely chopped onions
1½ pounds okra, sliced crosswise into ¼-inch pieces (about 3 cups)
½ cup finely diced green pepper
1 cup finely diced celery
2 cups dried lima beans
½ teaspoon salt
Freshly ground black pepper
6 cups cold water
1 pound (3 medium-sized) firm ripe tomatoes, cored and coarsely chopped
1½ cups corn kernels, cut from 3 medium-sized ears of corn, or substitute 1½ cups thoroughly defrosted frozen corn kernels

In a 10- to 12-inch skillet, fry the salt pork slices over moderately high heat, turning them frequently with tongs. When the pieces are crisp and brown and have rendered all their fat, transfer to paper towels to drain.

Add the chicken wings to the fat in the skillet and fry over moderately high heat for 2 to 3 minutes on each side, turning the wings with tongs, until they are golden brown. Transfer them to a plate and set aside. Add the onions, okra, green pepper, celery and lima beans to the skillet and, stirring frequently, cook for 3 to 5 minutes, until the vegetables have softened but have not yet begun to brown. Sprinkle with the ½ teaspoon of salt and a few grindings of black pepper, pour in the 6 cups of water, and return the salt pork and chicken wings to the pan, along with any juices that may have accumulated on the plate. Bring to a boil over high heat, then cover the pan tightly, reduce the heat to low, and simmer undisturbed for about 30 minutes. Add the tomatoes and corn and cook covered for 10 to 12 minutes, until the corn is tender. Taste for seasoning and transfer the stew to a heated casserole or deep serving bowl. Traditionally, okra stew is served over Southern dry rice (Recipe Index).

FISH & SHELLFISH

Red Snapper Citrus

To serve 4

½ cup finely chopped onions
¼ cup strained fresh orange juice
2 teaspoons finely grated fresh
   orange peel
1 teaspoon salt

Four 8- to 10-ounce red snapper
   fillets, with the skin left on
A pinch of ground nutmeg,
   preferably freshly grated
Freshly ground black pepper

Mix the onions, orange juice, orange peel and salt together in a shallow baking-serving dish large enough to hold the red snapper fillets in one layer. Add the fillets, turn them about in the orange mixture to moisten them evenly, then place them skin side up and set aside to marinate at room temperature for about 30 minutes.

Preheat the oven to 400°. Turn the fillets flesh side up and sprinkle them with a pinch of nutmeg and a few grindings of pepper. Basting the fish with the marinade from time to time, bake in the middle of the oven for 10 to 12 minutes, or until the fillets flake easily when prodded gently with a fork. Do not overcook. Serve the fish at once directly from the baking dish.

NOTE: Red snapper citrus can also be served chilled. If you prefer to present the fish cold, add 1 more teaspoon of salt to the marinade ingredients and follow the directions above for marinating and baking the fillets. Then cool them to room temperature, cover the dish tightly with foil or plastic wrap and refrigerate for 5 to 6 hours. The marinade will become a delicate jelly when it is chilled.

Pensacola Red Snapper

To serve 4

Four 8- to 10-ounce red snapper
    fillets, with the skin left on
1 teaspoon salt
Freshly ground black pepper
¼ cup strained fresh lemon juice
2 tablespoons olive oil

1½ teaspoons finely chopped garlic
1 teaspoon crumbled dried oregano
2 medium-sized firm ripe tomatoes,
    washed, cored and cut crosswise
    into ¼-inch-thick slices
1 tablespoon finely chopped fresh
    parsley

Preheat the oven to 400°. Pat the red snapper fillets completely dry with
paper towels and season them on both sides with the salt and a few grindings of pepper. Combine the lemon juice, olive oil, garlic and ½ teaspoon
of the oregano in a shallow baking-serving dish just large enough to hold
the fillets in one layer.

Stir the lemon juice mixture until the ingredients are well blended,
then add the fillets and turn them about to moisten them evenly. Arrange
the fillets skin side up, place the tomato slices over them, and sprinkle the
remaining ½ teaspoon of oregano on top.

Bake in the middle of the oven for 10 to 12 minutes, or until the fillets
flake easily when prodded gently with a fork. Sprinkle with the parsley
and serve the fillets at once, directly from the baking dish.

Southern Fried Fish

To serve 4

3 pounds catfish, porgy or
    butterfish, filleted but with skins
    left on
2 teaspoons salt

¼ teaspoon freshly ground black
    pepper
1 cup white cornmeal, preferably
    water-ground
Lard for deep frying

Pat the fish completely dry with paper towels. To keep the fish from curl-
ing up as they fry score the flesh side of each fillet with a small sharp
knife, making three diagonal slashes about 2 inches long and ⅛ inch
deep spaced an inch or so apart. Season the fillets on both sides with
the salt and pepper. Then dip them in the cornmeal to coat them evenly,
and gently shake off any excess meal.

In a heavy 12-inch skillet at least 2 inches deep, melt enough lard to
fill the pan to a depth of about ½ inch. Heat the fat until it is very hot
but not smoking, then add the fish. Fry the fillets for 4 minutes, turn
them with a slotted spatula and fry for 3 or 4 minutes longer, or until
they are richly and evenly browned. Arrange the fillets attractively on a
heated platter and serve at once. Traditionally, Southern fried fish is accompanied by coleslaw and hush puppies (Recipe Index).

Pompano Stuffed with Shrimp

To serve 4

5 tablespoons butter, softened, plus
   4 tablespoons butter
1 pound raw shrimp
4 to 6 medium-sized scallions,
   trimmed, washed and cut
   crosswise into ⅛-inch-thick
   rounds (about ½ cup) including
   2 inches of the green tops
1 cup fresh crumbs, made from day-
old homemade-type white bread,
   pulverized in a blender or finely
   shredded with a fork
¼ cup finely chopped fresh parsley
¼ cup pale dry sherry
Four 1½-pound pompanos,
   cleaned but with heads and tails
   left on
4 teaspoons salt
Freshly ground black pepper

Preheat the oven to 400°. With a pastry brush, spread 1 tablespoon of the softened butter evenly over the bottom of a large jelly-roll pan.

Shell the shrimp. Devein them by making a shallow incision down their backs with a small sharp knife and lifting out the black or white intestinal vein with the point of the knife. Drop the shrimp into enough lightly salted boiling water to immerse them completely and boil briskly, uncovered, for 3 minutes, or until they are firm and pink. Drain the shrimp, spread them on paper towels, and pat them completely dry with fresh towels. Then chop the shrimp coarsely and place them in a bowl.

In a heavy 8- to 10-inch skillet, melt 2 tablespoons of the butter over moderate heat. When the foam begins to subside, add the scallions and, stirring frequently, cook for 2 or 3 minutes, until they are soft and translucent but not brown. With a slotted spoon, transfer the scallions to the bowl of shrimp.

Melt the remaining 2 tablespoons of butter in the same skillet, add the bread crumbs and, stirring constantly, fry over moderate heat until the crumbs are crisp and golden brown. Scrape the entire contents of the skillet over the shrimp and scallions with a rubber spatula. Add the parsley and sherry, and toss all the stuffing ingredients together gently but thoroughly. Taste for seasoning.

Wash the pompanos under cold running water and pat them dry inside and out with paper towels. Season the cavities and skin of the fish with the salt and a few grindings of pepper. Spoon the shrimp stuffing into the cavities, dividing it evenly among them. Press the edges of the flaps together with your fingers.

Arrange the pompanos side by side on the buttered pan and brush the tops of the fish with the remaining 4 tablespoons of softened butter. Bake in the middle of the oven for 30 minutes, or until the pompanos feel firm when prodded gently with a finger. Arrange the fish attractively on a heated platter and serve at once.

Shrimp Pilau

To serve 4 to 6

6 medium-sized firm ripe tomatoes, or substitute 2 cups chopped drained canned tomatoes
2 cups uncooked long-grain white rice, not the converted variety
2 pounds medium-sized raw shrimp (about 21 to 25 to the pound)
8 slices bacon, cut into ¼-inch dice
2 cups finely chopped onions

3 cups chicken stock, fresh or canned
2 teaspoons Worcestershire sauce
1 teaspoon ground mace
½ teaspoon ground hot red pepper (cayenne)
2 teaspoons salt
2 tablespoons finely chopped fresh parsley

If you are using fresh tomatoes, prepare them in the following fashion: Drop 2 or 3 at a time into a pan of boiling water for 15 seconds. Run them under cold water and peel them with a small sharp knife. Cut out the stems, then slice each tomato in half crosswise. Squeeze the halves gently to remove the seeds and juice, then finely chop the tomatoes.

Place the rice in a sieve and wash it under cold running water, stirring the grains with a fork until the draining water runs clear. Set aside.

Peel the shrimp. Devein them by making a shallow incision down their backs with a small sharp knife and lifting out the black or white intestinal vein with the point of the knife. Wash the shrimp, then refrigerate until ready to use.

Preheat the oven to 350°. In a heavy 3- to 4-quart casserole, fry the bacon dice over moderate heat, stirring until they are crisp and brown and have rendered all their fat. With a slotted spoon, transfer the bacon to paper towels to drain.

Pour off all but about 3 tablespoons of the fat remaining in the casserole and drop in the onions. Stirring frequently, cook the onions over moderate heat for about 5 minutes, or until they are soft and translucent but not brown. Add the rice and stir until the grains glisten with the fat, then mix in the chicken stock or water, the tomatoes, Worcestershire, mace, red pepper and salt.

Bring to a boil over high heat, cover the casserole tightly and place it in the middle of the oven. Bake for 30 minutes, then add the shrimp and bacon and toss together gently but thoroughly. Cover tightly and continue to bake 10 minutes longer, or until the liquid in the pan has been absorbed and the shrimp are pink and tender.

Remove the casserole from the oven and set it aside without removing the cover for 10 minutes. Fluff the shrimp pilau with a fork, strew the parsley over the top and serve at once, directly from the casserole.

Oyster Croquettes

To make 12 croquettes

2 tablespoons butter
2 tablespoons flour
2 dozen oysters, drained and finely
    chopped (1½ cups), and ½
    cup of their liquor
½ cup milk
2 egg yolks
2 cups soft fresh crumbs, made

from homemade-type white bread,
    pulverized in a blender or finely
    shredded with a fork
¼ teaspoon crumbled dried thyme
¼ teaspoon ground hot red pepper
    (cayenne)
½ teaspoon salt
Vegetable oil for deep frying
Tartar sauce *(page 77)*

In a heavy 8- to 10-inch skillet, melt the butter over moderate heat. When the foam subsides, add the flour and mix well. Stirring the mixture constantly with a wire whisk, pour in the ½ cup of oyster liquor and the milk in a slow stream and cook over high heat until the sauce comes to a boil, thickens and is smooth. Reduce the heat to low and simmer for 2 to 3 minutes to remove any taste of the flour.

Beat the egg yolks lightly in a bowl, and mix in 1 or 2 tablespoons of the simmering sauce. Then pour the egg yolks into the sauce and stir with the whisk until it is smooth, but do not let it come anywhere near a boil or it will curdle.

With a rubber spatula, scrape the entire contents of the skillet into a bowl. Add the oysters, 1 cup of the bread crumbs, the thyme, red pepper and salt, and stir with a wooden spoon until the ingredients are thoroughly blended. Taste for seasoning, cover with foil or plastic wrap, and refrigerate for at least 1 hour.

To shape each croquette, scoop up about 3 tablespoons of the oyster mixture and pat into a ball about 2 inches in diameter. Roll the balls in the remaining cup of bread crumbs, arrange them side by side on a plate, and refrigerate for about 30 minutes to firm the coating.

Preheat the oven to its lowest setting. Line a shallow baking dish with a double thickness of paper towels and place it in the middle of the oven.

Pour the oil into a deep fryer or large heavy saucepan to a depth of 3 inches and heat to a temperature of 360° on a deep-frying thermometer.

Deep-fry the croquettes, 3 or 4 at a time, turning them frequently with a slotted spoon, for about 4 minutes, or until they are golden brown on all sides. As they brown, transfer them to the paper-lined dish and keep them warm in the oven while you deep-fry the rest.

Serve the oyster croquettes from a heated platter and present the tartar sauce separately in a bowl or sauceboat.

Steamed Crabs

To serve 8 to 12

⅔ cup coarse (kosher) salt
⅔ cup seafood seasoning *(page 76)*
2 cups cider vinegar

2 cups water
3 dozen live blue crabs, each about
    4 inches across

Mix the salt and seafood seasoning together in a bowl and set aside.

Set a rack in the bottom of a 10- to 12-quart enameled or stainless-steel pot 10 to 12 inches in diameter. Pour in the vinegar and water. Then place 6 or 7 crabs on the rack and sprinkle them evenly with 2 or 3 tablespoonfuls of the salt-seasoning mixture. Add another layer of 6 or 7 crabs, sprinkle them with several tablespoons of seasoning, and repeat 4 or 5 times, seasoning each layer of crabs as before.

Bring to a boil over high heat, cover tightly, reduce the heat to low, and steam the crabs for 20 minutes. Transfer the crabs to large heated platters with tongs and serve at once. Because these steamed crabs are so highly spiced, they are eaten without any accompaniment except, traditionally, tall glasses of cold beer.

Imperial Crab

To serve 4

2 teaspoons butter, softened, plus 2
    tablespoons butter, cut into bits
1 egg
2 tablespoons freshly made
    mayonnaise *(page 75)*, or
    substitute bottled mayonnaise
2 teaspoons Worcestershire sauce

½ teaspoon salt
¼ teaspoon ground white pepper
1 pound fresh, frozen or canned
    crabmeat, drained and picked
    over to remove all cartilage
¼ cup finely chopped green pepper
¼ cup finely chopped red pepper

Preheat the oven to 375°. With a pastry brush, spread the softened butter over 4 medium-sized natural or ceramic crab or scallop shells.

In a deep bowl, beat the egg lightly with a wire whisk. Add the mayonnaise, Worcestershire, salt and white pepper and whisk until the mixture is smooth. Then add the crabmeat and the green and red pepper and toss together gently but thoroughly with a rubber spatula.

Spoon the crab mixture into the buttered shells, dividing it evenly among them and mounding the centers slightly. Dot the tops with the butter bits. Bake in the upper third of the oven for 15 to 20 minutes, then slide them under a hot broiler for 30 seconds to brown the tops, if desired. Serve the imperial crab at once, directly from the shells.

1. To clean a live soft-shell crab, first freeze the crab briefly to numb it, then peel back the triangular apron.

2. With a small sharp knife, scrape out the stomach and intestines, which lie beneath the apron.

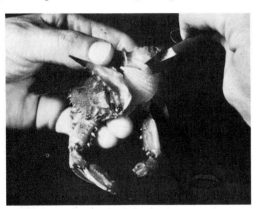

3. Turn over the crab, lift the shell at the tapering points on each end and insert knife into the grayish lungs

4. Clean out the spongy lungs, or "dead man's fingers," until the cartilage is completely exposed.

5. With a pair of sharp scissors, cut off and discard the head of the crab, just behind the eyes.

6. Squeeze the body and the sand sac will pop out of the head opening. Wash the crab in cold water.

Deep-fried Soft-Shell Crabs

To serve 4

12 soft-shell crabs, cleaned
  (opposite)
1 tablespoon salt
Freshly ground black pepper
1 cup flour
3 cups soft fresh crumbs made from

homemade-type white bread,
  pulverized in a blender or finely
  shredded with a fork
4 eggs
½ cup milk
Vegetable oil for deep frying
Tartar sauce (page 77)

Wash the crabs under cold running water, pat them completely dry with paper towels and season them on both sides with the salt and a few grindings of pepper.

Spread the flour and bread crumbs on separate plates or pieces of wax paper. In a wide bowl, beat the eggs lightly with a wire whisk or rotary beater, then beat in the milk.

One at a time, dip a crab into the flour to coat both sides. Shake off the excess flour, immerse the crab in the egg-milk mixture, then coat it with the crumbs, covering the crab completely.

When all of the crabs have been floured, dipped in the egg mixture, and breaded, arrange them side by side on 1 or 2 large baking sheets and refrigerate them for at least 20 minutes to firm the coating.

Preheat the oven to its lowest setting. Then line a large shallow baking dish with a double thickness of paper towels and place it on the middle shelf of the oven.

Pour vegetable oil into a deep fryer or large heavy saucepan to a depth of 3 inches and heat until the oil reaches a temperature of 360° on a deep-frying thermometer.

Deep-fry the crabs, 2 or 3 at a time. Turn them occasionally with tongs or a slotted spoon and fry them about 5 minutes, or until they are golden brown. As they brown, transfer them to the lined dish and keep them warm in the oven while you deep-fry the rest.

Arrange the crabs attractively on a heated platter and serve them at once, accompanied by a bowl of tartar sauce.

Fried Soft-Shell Crabs

To serve 4

12 soft-shell crabs, cleaned (page 32)	3 to 6 tablespoons vegetable oil
1 tablespoon salt	6 tablespoons finely chopped fresh parsley
1 cup flour	3 tablespoons strained fresh lemon
11 tablespoons butter	juice

Preheat the oven to its lowest setting. Then line a large shallow baking dish with a double thickness of paper towels and place it on the middle shelf of the oven.

Wash the crabs under cold running water, pat them completely dry with paper towels and season them evenly with the salt. One at a time, dip the crabs in the flour to coat both sides and shake vigorously to remove the excess flour.

In a heavy 10- to 12-inch skillet, melt 3 tablespoons of the butter with 3 tablespoons of the oil over moderate heat until the foam begins to subside. Fry the crabs, 2 or 3 at a time, for about 5 minutes, turning them frequently with tongs and regulating the heat so that they color richly and evenly without burning. As they brown, transfer the crabs to the lined dish to drain and keep them warm in the oven while you fry the rest. Add the remaining 3 tablespoons of oil to the skillet, a spoonful at a time, if necessary.

Just before serving, melt the remaining 8 tablespoons of butter over moderate heat in a 6- to 8-inch skillet, regulating the heat and stirring to prevent the butter from browning. Remove the pan from the heat and stir in the chopped parsley and lemon juice.

Arrange the crabs attractively on a heated platter and dribble a few tablespoonfuls of the butter sauce over them. Present the rest of the butter separately in a small bowl or sauceboat.

Crab Cakes

To serve 4

1 egg
2 tablespoons freshly made
  mayonnaise *(page 75)*, or
  substitute bottled mayonnaise
½ teaspoon dry mustard
⅛ teaspoon ground hot red pepper
  (cayenne)
⅛ teaspoon Tabasco
½ teaspoon salt
½ teaspoon ground white pepper
1 pound fresh, frozen or canned

crabmeat, drained and picked
  over to remove all cartilage
3 tablespoons finely chopped fresh
  parsley
1½ tablespoons fresh crumbs
  made from unsalted soda
  crackers, pulverized in a blender
  or with a rolling pin
Vegetable oil for deep frying
1 lemon, cut into 8 wedges
Tartar sauce *(page 77)*

In a deep bowl, beat the egg lightly with a wire whisk. Add the mayonnaise, mustard, red pepper, Tabasco, salt and white pepper and whisk until the mixture is smooth. Then add the crabmeat, parsley and cracker crumbs and toss together all the ingredients with a fork. Divide the mixture into 8 equal portions, and shape each of these into a ball about 2 inches in diameter. Wrap in wax paper and chill the cakes for 30 minutes.

Pour oil into a deep fryer or large heavy saucepan to a depth of 3 inches and heat the oil to a temperature of 375° on a deep-frying thermometer.

Deep-fry the crab cakes 4 at a time, turning them with a slotted spoon for 2 or 3 minutes until they are golden on all sides. As they brown, transfer them to paper towels to drain. Arrange the crab cakes with the lemon wedges on a heated platter. Serve at once, accompanied by the tartar sauce in a separate bowl.

Crab Omelet

To serve 2

2 tablespoons butter
3 tablespoons finely chopped celery
2 tablespoons finely cut fresh chives
1 teaspoon freshly made catsup
  (page 76), or substitute 1
  teaspoon tomato purée
½ teaspoon pale dry sherry
¼ teaspoon Worcestershire sauce
¼ teaspoon sugar
Freshly ground black pepper
¼ pound (about ½ cup) fresh,
  frozen or canned crabmeat,
  thoroughly drained and picked
  over to remove all bits of
  cartilage
3 eggs
1 teaspoon salt

In a heavy 8- to 10-inch skillet, preferably one with a nonstick cooking surface, melt the butter over moderate heat. Drop in the celery and chives and, stirring constantly, cook for about 5 minutes, until they have wilted but have not browned. Stir in the catsup or tomato purée, the sherry, Worcestershire, sugar and a few grindings of pepper. Then add the crab-meat and mix well.

With a table fork, beat the eggs and salt lightly in a small bowl. Pour the eggs over the crab mixture and stir them together with the flat of the fork. Sliding the skillet back and forth occasionally to prevent the omelet from sticking to the pan, cook over moderate heat for 2 to 3 minutes, until the omelet is firm to the touch.

Place the skillet beside a heated serving plate, tilt the pan, and let the omelet slowly slip out. Serve at once.

Maryland Deviled Crab

To serve 4

2 teaspoons butter, softened, plus 4 tablespoons butter

6 tablespoons soft fresh crumbs made from homemade-type white bread, pulverized in a blender or finely shredded with a fork

2 tablespoons flour

¾ cup milk

2 hard-cooked eggs, the yolks rubbed through a fine sieve with the back of a spoon, and the whites finely chopped

2 teaspoons strained fresh lemon juice

1 teaspoon Worcestershire sauce

¼ teaspoon Tabasco

½ teaspoon dry mustard

¼ teaspoon ground hot red pepper (cayenne)

1 teaspoon salt

Freshly ground black pepper

1 pound fresh, frozen or canned lump crabmeat, thoroughly drained and picked over to remove all bits of cartilage

3 tablespoons finely chopped green pepper

Preheat the oven to 375°. With a pastry brush, spread the 2 teaspoons of softened butter over the bottoms of 4 medium-sized natural or ceramic crab or scallop shells.

In a heavy 8- to 10-inch skillet, melt 2 tablespoons of butter over moderate heat. Drop in the bread crumbs and stir until they are crisp and golden. With a rubber spatula, scrape the entire contents of the pan into a small bowl and set aside.

In the same skillet, melt the remaining 2 tablespoons of butter over moderate heat. When the foam begins to subside, add the flour and mix well. Stirring the mixture constantly with a wire whisk, pour in the milk in a slow stream and cook over high heat until the sauce comes to a boil, thickens and is smooth. Then reduce the heat to low and simmer the sauce for 2 or 3 minutes.

Remove the skillet from the heat and stir the sieved egg yolks into the sauce. When they are well incorporated, beat in the lemon juice, Worcestershire sauce, Tabasco, dry mustard, red pepper, salt and a few grindings of black pepper. Now add the crabmeat, chopped green pepper and chopped egg whites and toss the mixture together gently but thoroughly with a table fork. Taste for seasoning.

Spoon the crab mixture into the buttered shells, dividing it evenly among them and slightly mounding the centers. Sprinkle the reserved crumbs over the tops.

Bake the deviled crab in the upper third of the oven for 15 to 20 minutes, then slide them under the broiler for 30 seconds to brown the tops, if desired. Serve at once, directly from the shells.

POULTRY & GAME

Maryland Fried Chicken with Cream Gravy

Fried chicken is as Southern as a mint julep—and stirs as many debates. Almost every cook uses a different recipe; there is no King James version. In Maryland, traditionally the bird is seasoned and floured before frying, and it is served with gravy made from the pan drippings. Even so, Marylanders themselves do not agree on whether to pour the gravy over the chicken or present it in a sauceboat. Below and on the following pages are recipes for four of the best ways of preparing fried chicken.

To serve 4

	2½ teaspoons salt
1½ to 2 pounds lard, or substitute	Freshly ground black pepper
3 to 4 cups vegetable oil	½ cup plus 2 tablespoons flour
A 2½- to 3-pound chicken, cut	1 cup milk
into 8 serving pieces	1 cup heavy cream

Preheat the oven to its lowest setting. Then line a large shallow baking dish with a double thickness of paper towels and place the dish on the middle shelf of the oven.

Melt 1½ pounds of the lard over high heat in a heavy 10-inch skillet at least 2 inches deep or in a large heavy saucepan. When melted the fat should be about 1 inch deep; if necessary, add more lard. Or pour the vegetable oil into a comparable skillet or saucepan to a depth of 1 inch. Heat the fat until it reaches a temperature of 375° on a deep-frying thermometer, or until it is very hot but not smoking.

Pat the pieces of chicken completely dry with paper towels and season them on all sides with 2 teaspoons of the salt and a few grindings of pepper. Dip each piece of chicken in ½ cup of the flour, turn to coat it evenly, and vigorously shake off the excess flour.

Fry the chicken legs and drumsticks, starting the pieces skin side down and turning them frequently with tongs, for about 12 minutes, or until they color richly and evenly. To be sure that the bird is cooked to the proper degree of doneness, lift a piece from the pan and pierce it deeply with the point of a small skewer or sharp knife. The juice that trickles out should be clear yellow; if it is still tinged with pink, fry the pieces for 2 or 3 minutes more. As they brown, drain the pieces of chicken in the paper-lined dish and keep them warm in the oven.

Then fry the wings and breasts, in two batches if necessary to avoid crowding the pan. The white meat pieces should be fully cooked in 7 or 8 minutes. When they are brown, add them to the dish in the oven.

Pour off all but a thin film of fat from the pan and in its place add the remaining 2 tablespoons of flour. Mix well. Then, stirring the mixture constantly with a wire whisk, pour in the milk and cream in a thin stream and cook over high heat until the gravy comes to a boil, thickens lightly and is smooth. Reduce the heat to low and simmer for 2 or 3 minutes to remove the taste of flour. Add the remaining ½ teaspoon of salt and a few grindings of pepper and taste for seasoning.

Arrange the chicken on a platter and pour the cream gravy over it, or ladle the gravy into a bowl or sauceboat, arrange the chicken on a heated platter and serve at once. Maryland fried chicken is traditionally accompanied by fried biscuits *(Recipe Index)*. If you wish to serve the biscuits, fry them in the hot fat after the chicken and keep them warm in the oven in the same lined baking dish while you prepare the gravy.

Oven-fried Chicken

Fried chicken is the mainstay of a Southern church supper or family reunion, but frying enough chicken for a crowd can be tedious and time consuming. The following recipe can be used where large quantities of chicken are required; although the birds are baked in the oven, their texture and flavor are similar to those of fried chicken.

To serve 12 to 16

	2 tablespoons paprika
Four 2½- to 3-pound chickens,	Freshly ground black pepper
each cut into 8 pieces	8 tablespoons (1 quarter-pound
2 tablespoons salt	stick) unsalted butter, cut into bits

Preheat the oven to 400°. Wash the chicken pieces under cold running water and pat them thoroughly dry with paper towels. Sprinkle the pieces on all sides with the salt, paprika and several grindings of black pepper. Spread the pieces out in one layer in one or more shallow baking pans. Scatter half of the butter bits evenly over the chicken and cover the pan or pans securely with a large sheet of aluminum foil. Bake in the center of the oven for 20 minutes, then remove the foil, raise the oven temperature to 450°, and bake undisturbed for 30 minutes longer. Turn over the chicken pieces with tongs, sprinkle with the remaining butter bits, and bake uncovered for an additional 30 minutes. Serve the chicken either hot or at room temperature, accompanied, if you like, by potato salad or cole slaw with boiled dressing *(Recipe Index)*.

Kentucky Fried Chicken

To serve 4

2 to 4 pounds lard
A 2½- to 3-pound chicken, cut
   into 8 serving pieces
2 teaspoons salt
Freshly ground black pepper
1 egg, lightly beaten and combined
   with ½ cup milk
1 cup flour

Preheat the oven to its lowest setting. Then line a large shallow baking dish with paper towels and place it in the center of the oven.

Melt 2 pounds of the lard over high heat in a deep fryer or large heavy saucepan. When melted, the fat should be 1½ to 2 inches deep; add more lard if necessary. Heat the lard to a temperature of 375° on a deep-frying thermometer, or until it is very hot but not smoking.

Pat the pieces of chicken completely dry with paper towels and season them on all sides with the salt and a few grindings of pepper. Immerse the chicken pieces one at a time in the egg-and-milk mixture, then dip them in the flour and turn to coat them lightly but evenly.

Fry the chicken legs and drumsticks, stacking them skin side down and turning them frequently with tongs for about 12 minutes, or until they color richly and evenly. As they brown, transfer them to the paper-lined dish and keep them warm in the oven. Then fry the wings and breast, separately if necessary to avoid overcrowding the pan. The white meat will be fully cooked in 7 or 8 minutes.

When all the pieces are fried, mound the chicken attractively on a heated platter and serve at once.

Southern Fried Chicken with Onion Gravy

To serve 4

A 2½- to 3-pound chicken, cut
  into 8 serving pieces
2½ teaspoons salt
Freshly ground black pepper
1 cup plus 2 tablespoons flour

1½ to 2 pounds lard
2 medium-sized onions, peeled and
  cut crosswise into ⅛-inch-thick
  slices (2 cups)
2 cups water
1 tablespoon distilled white vinegar

Preheat the oven to its lowest setting. Then line a large shallow baking dish with paper towels and place it in the center of the oven.

Pat the pieces of chicken completely dry with paper towels and season them on all sides with 2 teaspoons of the salt and a few grindings of pepper. One at a time dip the pieces in 1 cup of the flour and turn to coat them evenly. Shake each piece vigorously to remove the excess flour.

Melt 1½ pounds of the lard over high heat in a heavy 12-inch skillet at least 2 inches deep and equipped with a tightly fitting lid. When melted, the fat should be about ½ inch deep; add more lard if necessary. When the lard is very hot but not smoking, place the pieces of chicken skin side down in the skillet and set the lid on top. Fry over high heat for 5 minutes, turn the pieces of chicken with tongs and continue to fry, still tightly covered, for 4 to 5 minutes longer, or until the chicken is richly and evenly browned on both sides.

Transfer the chicken to the paper-lined dish and keep it warm in the oven while you prepare the onion gravy. Pour off all but about 1 tablespoon of the fat remaining in the skillet and in its place add the onions. Sprinkle them with the remaining 2 tablespoons of flour and, stirring frequently, cook over high heat for 3 or 4 minutes, or until the onions are soft and golden brown. Stirring them constantly with a spoon, pour in the water in a slow stream and cook until the gravy comes to a boil, thickens and is smooth. Stir in the vinegar, the remaining ½ teaspoon of salt and a few grindings of pepper. Remove the skillet from the heat and taste the gravy for seasoning.

To serve, arrange the chicken attractively on a heated platter and pour the onion gravy over it. Or, more traditionally, mound Southern dry rice (Recipe Index) in a serving bowl, pour the onion gravy over the rice, and serve the gravy-smothered rice with the chicken.

To prepare stuffed corn, remove the cob from the husk and cut off the kernels. Stuff the husk with the chicken mixture, then tie with cornhusk strip.

Chicken-stuffed Corn

To serve 4

2 pounds chicken breasts
4 teaspoons salt
Freshly ground black pepper
4 cups water
6 slices lean bacon

8 medium-sized unhusked ears of
  fresh corn
4 eggs, lightly beaten
½ cup heavy cream
¼ cup finely chopped ripe black
  olives

Place the chicken breasts in a heavy 2- to 3-quart saucepan, add 2 tea-spoons of the salt and a few grindings of pepper, and pour in 4 cups of water. Bring to a boil over high heat, reduce the heat to low, cover the pan partially and simmer for about 20 minutes, or until the chicken feels firm when pressed with your finger. Drain the chicken; strain the cooking stock and reserve it for another use. With a small knife, remove the skin and bones from the breasts and discard them. Cut the chicken into ½-inch pieces and set aside.

Meanwhile, in a heavy 10- to 12-inch skillet, fry the bacon slices over moderate heat, turning them frequently with tongs until they are crisp and brown. Transfer the bacon to paper towels to drain, then crumble it into small pieces.

Shuck one ear of corn at a time, turning the husks back carefully so that they remain intact. Break off each cob at its base, pull out the corn silk, and set the husks and silk aside.

With a sharp knife, slice the kernels from the corn into a deep bowl, taking care not to cut too deeply into the cob. Add the eggs, cream, the remaining 2 teaspoons of salt and a liberal grinding of pepper to the corn kernels and mix well. Stir in the chicken, bacon and the black olives. Taste for seasoning.

To stuff each cornhusk, stand it on its base in a tall, straight-sided tumbler 3 or 4 inches in diameter as shown left. Separate the tops of the leaves and spread them apart so that the lower half of the cornhusk forms a boatlike shell. Spoon about ½ cup of the chicken mixture into the cornhusk shell, then draw the tops of the leaves together again to enclose the stuffing completely. Secure the stuffing by tying a few strands of corn silk, husk, or kitchen cord snugly around the end of the cornhusk.

Place the stuffed cornhusks one on top of the other in a large colander set inside a deep pot. Pour enough water into the pot to come to within an inch of the bottom of the colander, and bring to a boil over high heat. Cover the pot tightly, reduce the heat to low, and steam the chicken-stuffed corn for 20 minutes. With tongs, arrange the corn on a heated platter, and serve it at once.

Barbecued Quail

To serve 4

1 cup finely chopped onions	¼ teaspoon Tabasco
¼ cup dark brown sugar	½ cup catsup, preferably freshly
¼ cup distilled white vinegar	made *(page 76)*
¼ cup Worcestershire sauce	3 tablespoons vegetable oil or lard
1 teaspoon dry mustard	4 oven-ready quail

To prepare the barbecue sauce, combine the onions, sugar, vinegar, Worcestershire, mustard, Tabasco and catsup in a 1- to 1½-quart enameled or stainless-steel saucepan. Stirring constantly with a wooden spoon, bring the sauce to a boil over high heat. Reduce the heat to low and simmer uncovered for 5 to 8 minutes, until the onions are soft.

Heat the oil or lard in a heavy 10- to 12-inch enameled or stainless-steel skillet set over high heat. When the fat is very hot but not smoking, add the quail and fry for 2 to 3 minutes on each side, turning the birds with tongs. When they are golden brown, remove the skillet from the heat.

With a bulb baster, remove and discard all the fat in the pan. Pour the barbecue sauce over the quail and partially cover the skillet. Simmer the quail for 15 to 20 minutes over low heat, basting them with the sauce every 5 minutes or so. To test the quail for doneness, pierce a thigh with the point of a small sharp knife. The juice that trickles out should be pale yellow; if pink, cook for 5 to 10 minutes more. Transfer the quail to a heated platter, pour the sauce over them, and serve at once, accompanied, if you like, by Southern dry rice or Jefferson rice *(Recipe Index)*.

Roast Wild Duck

To serve 6 to 8

½ cup bacon fat, or substitute ½	¼-inch-thick slices
cup vegetable oil	2 large firm ripe apples, unpeeled
4 tablespoons butter	but cored and cut into ½-inch-
Four 1½- to 2-pound oven-ready	thick wedges
wild ducks (such as mallard	4 medium-sized celery stalks,
or teal)	trimmed of all leaves, cut
Salt	lengthwise in half and crosswise
Freshly ground black pepper	into 1½-inch-long strips
2 navel oranges, cut crosswise into	¼ cup pale dry sherry

Preheat the oven to 450°. In a small pan, melt the bacon fat and butter over low heat. Remove the pan from the heat and set aside.

Wash the ducks under cold running water and pat them dry inside and out with paper towels. Season the cavities and the skin with salt and a few grindings of pepper. Combine the oranges, apples, celery and sherry in a bowl and toss together. Then fill the cavity of each bird with the fruit-and-celery mixture and close the openings by lacing them with skewers and kitchen cord or sewing them with heavy thread. Truss the birds and fasten the neck skin to the back with small skewers.

Place the ducks on their side on a rack in a shallow roasting pan. With a pastry brush, spread about 2 tablespoons of the bacon-fat-and-butter mixture evenly over each bird. Roast in the middle of the oven for 15 minutes, then turn the duck over onto the other side and brush them again with the melted fat. Roast for another 15 minutes. Reduce the oven temperature to 350°. Turn the ducks breast side up and brush them with fat again. Roast for about 1 hour longer, turning the birds every 15 minutes and brushing them each time with the remaining fat. To test for doneness, pierce the thigh of a duck with the point of a small sharp knife. The juice that trickles out should be pale yellow; if it is still tinged with pink, roast the birds for 5 to 10 minutes longer.

Transfer the ducks to a cutting board and, with poultry scissors, remove the trussing strings and cut each bird in half lengthwise. Discard the stuffing. Arrange the duck halves on a large heated platter and serve at once, accompanied, if you like, by pepper relish *(Recipe Index)*.

Chicken-Liver Casserole with Mushrooms and Eggplant

To serve 4 to 6

3 quarts water	2 eggs
4 teaspoons salt	½ cup heavy cream
2 medium-sized eggplants (about 1 pound each), peeled and cut into 1½- to 2-inch cubes (8 cups)	¼ teaspoon ground nutmeg
	Freshly ground black pepper
	½ cup soft fresh crumbs, made from homemade-type white bread, pulverized in a blender or finely shredded with a fork
4 tablespoons butter plus 1 tablespoon butter, cut into bits	
½ pound chicken livers	
1 pound mushrooms, thinly sliced	½ cup grated Parmesan cheese

Preheat the oven to 350°. In a 6- to 8-quart casserole, combine 3 quarts of water and 3 teaspoons of the salt, and bring to a boil over high heat. Drop in the eggplant, reduce the heat to moderate, and cook uncovered for 15 to 20 minutes, or until the eggplant is tender enough to offer no resistance when pierced with the tip of a sharp knife. Drain the eggplant in a colander and place the cubes in a large mixing bowl. Then, with a potato masher or fork, mash them to a smooth purée and set aside.

Melt the 4 tablespoons of butter in a heavy 10- to 12-inch skillet set over moderate heat. When the foam begins to subside, add the chicken livers and fry them for 3 or 4 minutes on each side, tossing and turning them with a wooden spoon or spatula. When they are a light golden brown, remove the livers from the pan with a slotted spoon and chop them as fine as possible. Add them to the bowl of puréed eggplant.

Continued on next page   45

In the fat remaining in the skillet, fry the mushrooms for 4 or 5 minutes over moderate heat, stirring frequently. When they are lightly colored, transfer the mushrooms to the purée and chicken livers.

In a small mixing bowl, beat the eggs lightly with a wire whisk or fork, then beat in the heavy cream, nutmeg, the remaining teaspoon of salt and several grindings of black pepper. Pour the contents of the bowl over the eggplant, livers and mushrooms. Toss with a large spoon until the ingredients are thoroughly combined. Taste for seasoning, and spoon the mixture into a 1-quart baking-and-serving casserole, smoothing the surface with a rubber spatula. Combine the bread crumbs and grated cheese and sprinkle them evenly over the top. Dot with the tablespoon of butter bits and bake the casserole in the center of the oven for 25 to 30 minutes, or until the crust is golden brown. Serve at once, directly from the casserole.

Roast Turkey with Cornbread, Sausage and Pecan Stuffing

To serve 8 to 12

A 12- to 14-pound oven-ready turkey, thoroughly defrosted if frozen, and the turkey liver, finely chopped
1½ teaspoons salt
Freshly ground black pepper
1 pound breakfast-type sausage meat, preferably freshly made *(½ the recipe for country-style sausage, page 8)*
1½ cups finely chopped onions
½ cup finely chopped celery
5 cups coarsely crumbled, cooled cornbread *(page 88)*

1½ cups (about ½ pound) coarsely chopped pecans
¼ cup pale dry sherry
¼ cup milk
¼ cup finely chopped fresh parsley
½ teaspoon crumbled dried thyme
¼ teaspoon ground nutmeg, preferably freshly grated
12 tablespoons butter, melted
½ cup coarsely chopped onions
3 tablespoons flour
1½ cups turkey stock *(see note, opposite)*, or substitute fresh or canned chicken stock

Preheat the oven to 400°. Pat the turkey completely dry inside and out with paper towels. Rub the cavity with 1 teaspoon of the salt and a few grindings of pepper, and set the bird aside.

In a heavy 10- to 12-inch ungreased skillet, fry the sausage meat over moderate heat, stirring frequently and mashing the meat with the back of a fork to break up any lumps as they form. When no trace of pink remains, scoop up the sausage meat with a slotted spoon and transfer it to a fine sieve to drain.

Pour off all but a few tablespoonfuls of the sausage fat remaining in the skillet and add the finely chopped onions and celery. Stirring frequently, cook over moderate heat for about 5 minutes, or until the vegetables are soft but not brown. With a slotted spoon, transfer them to a deep bowl. Add the drained sausage meat, the cornbread, pecans, sherry, milk, turkey liver, parsley, thyme, nutmeg, the remaining ½ teaspoon of salt and a few grindings of pepper, and toss together gently but thoroughly. Taste for seasoning and let the stuffing cool to room temperature.

Fill both the breast and the neck cavity of the turkey with the stuffing and close the openings by lacing them with small skewers and kitchen cord or sewing them with heavy white thread. Truss the bird securely.

With a pastry brush, spread the melted butter evenly over the entire surface of the turkey. Place the bird on its side on a rack set in a large shallow roasting pan and roast in the middle of the oven for 15 minutes. Turn the turkey on its other side, and roast for 15 minutes more.

Then reduce the oven temperature to 325°, place the turkey breast side down, basting it every 15 minutes or so with the juices that have accumulated in the bottom of the pan. Now turn the bird breast side up and scatter the coarsely chopped onions around it. Roast for about 1 hour longer, basting the turkey every 15 minutes or so with the pan juices.

To test for doneness, pierce the thigh of the turkey with the tip of a small sharp knife. The juice that trickles out should be a clear yellow; if it is slightly pink, return the bird to the oven and roast for another 5 to 10 minutes. Transfer the turkey to a heated platter and let it rest for 10 minutes or so for easier carving.

Meanwhile, skim off and discard all but a thin film of fat from the roasting pan. Stir the flour into the fat and cook over moderate heat for 2 or 3 minutes, meanwhile scraping in the brown particles clinging to the bottom and sides of the pan.

Pour in the turkey or chicken stock and, stirring constantly with a wire whisk, cook over high heat until the sauce comes to a boil, thickens and is smooth. Reduce the heat to low and simmer uncovered for about 5 minutes, then strain the gravy through a fine sieve into a serving bowl or sauceboat. Taste for seasoning. Carve the turkey at the table and present the gravy separately.

NOTE: If you would like to prepare turkey stock, start about 2 hours before you prepare the stuffing. Combine the turkey neck, gizzard, and heart, 1 scraped chopped carrot, 1 peeled and quartered onion, 4 fresh parsley sprigs, 1 small bay leaf, 1 teaspoon of salt and 4 cups of water in a saucepan. Bring to a boil over high heat, reduce the heat to low and simmer partially covered for 1½ hours. Strain the liquid through a fine sieve into a bowl and skim as much fat as possible from the surface. There should be about 2 cups of stock.

Jellied Chicken

To serve 6 to 8

A 3- to 3½-pound chicken, cut
    into 6 or 8 pieces
5⅓ cups cold water
1 medium-sized onion, peeled and
    thinly sliced
1 large carrot, scraped and thinly
    sliced, plus ⅓ cup finely grated
    scraped carrot
2 celery stalks, trimmed of all leaves
    and coarsely chopped

1 small bay leaf
1 tablespoon salt
6 whole black peppercorns
2 envelopes unflavored gelatin
½ cup sour cream
½ cup freshly made mayonnaise
    (page 75), or substitute
    unsweetened bottled mayonnaise
2 teaspoons Worcestershire sauce
3 tablespoons finely chopped fresh
    parsley

Combine the chicken and 5 cups of water in a heavy 4- to 5-quart saucepan and bring to a boil over high heat, meanwhile skimming off the
foam and scum as they rise to the surface. Add the onion, sliced carrot, celery, bay leaf, salt and peppercorns, lower the heat, and simmer partially
covered for 35 to 40 minutes, or until the chicken is tender but still intact.

Meanwhile, pour the remaining ⅓ cup of cold water into a small
bowl and sprinkle the gelatin over it. Set the gelatin aside to soften.

When the chicken is done, transfer the pieces to a plate. With a small
sharp knife remove and discard the skin and bones, cut the meat into
½-inch cubes, and set aside.

Strain the cooking liquid through a fine sieve, pressing down hard on
the vegetables with the back of a spoon to extract all their juices before discarding the pulp. Return the strained stock to the saucepan, add the
gelatin, and cook over low heat, stirring constantly, until the gelatin dissolves. Pour the stock into a bowl and cool to room temperature.

In a deep bowl, stir the sour cream, mayonnaise and Worcestershire together with a wire whisk until they are well blended. Whisking constantly,
pour in the cooled stock in a slow, thin stream and continue to beat until
the mixture is smooth. Stir in the grated carrot and parsley, taste for seasoning, then ladle about 1 cup into a 1½-quart rectangular or square baking dish at least 1½ inches deep. With a rubber spatula spread the
vegetables evenly over the bottom of the dish and refrigerate for about
1 hour, or until the jellied stock is firm to the touch.

Stir the reserved chicken cubes into the gelatin mixture remaining in
the bowl, then ladle it over the jellied stock in the baking dish. Spread
out the chicken with the spatula, cover the dish with foil, and refrigerate
for 6 to 8 hours, or until the jellied chicken is firm.

To unmold and serve the jellied chicken, run a thin-bladed knife
around the edges of the dish to loosen the sides, then dip the bottom briefly into hot water. Place a chilled serving plate upside down over the dish
and, grasping plate and dish together firmly, quickly invert them. Rap
the plate sharply on a table. The jellied chicken should slide out easily.

Roast Loin of Pork with Sweet Potatoes and Apples

To serve 6

A 5- to 5½-pound pork loin in
    1 piece, with the backbone sawed
    through lengthwise but left
    attached and tied to the loin in
    4 or 5 places with kitchen cord
1 teaspoon salt

½ teaspoon freshly ground black
    pepper
3 sweet potatoes (about 2 pounds),
    peeled and cut in half lengthwise
6 tart firm red apples, cored
1 teaspoon ground cinnamon, mixed
    with ¼ cup light brown sugar

Preheat the oven to 350°. Rub the pork loin on all sides with the salt and pepper, and place it fat side up in a large roasting pan. Insert the tip of a meat thermometer horizontally at least 2 inches into one side of the loin. Be sure that the tip of the thermometer does not touch any fat or bone.

Roast the loin undisturbed in the middle of the oven for 45 minutes, then arrange the halved sweet potatoes around it and roast for 15 minutes longer. Now intersect the potatoes with the apples and fill their hollows with the cinnamon-and-sugar mixture. Roast for another 30 minutes, or until the meat thermometer indicates a temperature of 165°.

Transfer the roast pork to a heated platter and let it rest for about 10 minutes for easier carving. Surround the roast with the sweet potatoes and apples. Skim and discard the fat from the juices in the roasting pan and serve the gravy in a heated sauceboat.

Barbecued Spareribs

To serve 4 to 6

1 cup finely chopped onions
1 cup freshly made catsup (*page 76*) or 1 cup peach preserves (depending on whether you prefer a very spicy or slightly sweet sauce)
¼ cup dark brown sugar
¼ cup distilled white vinegar

¼ cup Worcestershire sauce
1 teaspoon dry mustard
¼ teaspoon Tabasco
4 pounds spareribs, in 2 or 3 pieces, trimmed of excess fat
2 teaspoons salt
Freshly ground black pepper
2 lemons, cut crosswise into ¼-inch-thick slices

Preheat the oven to 400°. While it is heating, prepare the barbecue basting sauce: combine the onions, catsup or peach preserves, brown sugar, vinegar, Worcestershire, mustard and Tabasco in a 1- to 1½-quart enameled or stainless-steel saucepan. Stirring constantly with a wooden spoon, bring the sauce to a boil over high heat. Reduce the heat to low and simmer for 4 or 5 minutes until the onions are soft.

Arrange the spareribs, flesh side up, side by side on a rack set in a large shallow roasting pan and sprinkle them with the salt and a few grindings of pepper. With a pastry brush, spread about ½ cup of the basting sauce evenly over the ribs and lay the lemon slices on top. Bake uncovered in the middle of the oven for about 1½ hours, brushing the ribs 3 or 4 more times with the remaining sauce. The ribs are done if the meat shows no resistance when pierced deeply with the point of a small skewer or sharp knife.

Arrange the barbecued spareribs on a heated platter and serve at once.

Spiced Beef Round

1 cup dark brown sugar
1 cup salt
1 tablespoon ground allspice
1 tablespoon freshly ground black pepper
2 teaspoons ground ginger
1 teaspoon ground nutmeg
1 teaspoon ground cinnamon

1 teaspoon ground hot red pepper (cayenne)
A 4- to 5-pound beef round roast about 3 inches thick, tied securely in 3 or 4 places
¼ pound beef suet, cut into 8 or 9 strips each 3 inches long and ¼ inch wide

Starting about 2 weeks ahead, combine the brown sugar, salt, allspice, black pepper, ginger, nutmeg, cinnamon and red pepper in a large bowl. Mix thoroughly, then place the beef in the bowl and, with your fingers, rub the sugar-and-spice mixture into all sides of the meat. Cover the bowl tightly with foil or plastic wrap and marinate in the refrigerator for 2 weeks, turning the meat over every day and basting it with the liquid that will accumulate in the bowl.

Preheat the oven to 275°. Transfer the meat to a plate and reserve the marinade. With a larding needle or sharp skewer, make 8 or 9 evenly spaced holes through the beef roast from top to bottom and insert a strip of suet in each one. Place the beef on a rack in a large heavy casserole equipped with a tightly fitting lid. Pour ¾ cup of the marinade down the sides of the casserole. Then cover tightly with the lid and braise in the middle of the oven for 3½ hours, or until the beef is tender and shows no resistance when pierced deeply with a large two-pronged fork.

Transfer the beef to a platter and cool to room temperature. Cover with foil or plastic wrap, and refrigerate the beef for at least 8 hours, or until it is thoroughly chilled and firm.

Spiced beef round is a traditional Christmas dish in Virginia and Tennessee. This version, from Virginia, is served sliced paper-thin and accompanied by beaten biscuits (*Recipe Index*).

Mobile Thyme Tongue

To serve 6 to 8

A 4-pound fresh beef tongue	1 medium-sized garlic clove, peeled
2 cups distilled white vinegar	and cut crosswise into ⅛-inch-
1 cup dry red wine	thick slices
1 cup dark brown sugar	1 tablespoon dry mustard
2 medium-sized onions, peeled and	1 teaspoon crumbled dried thyme
cut into ¼-inch-thick slices	1 tablespoon salt

With a small sharp skewer, pierce completely through the beef tongue in at least a dozen places. Then set the tongue aside in an enameled casserole just large enough to hold it comfortably.

Combine the vinegar, wine, sugar, onions, garlic, mustard, thyme and salt in a 2-quart saucepan. Bring to a boil over high heat, stirring until the sugar and mustard dissolve. Immediately pour over the tongue and turn the meat about to moisten it evenly. Refrigerate uncovered and when the marinade is cool, cover the casserole with its lid. Let the tongue marinate in the refrigerator for 24 hours, turning it over two or three times.

Preheat the oven to 300°. Bring the tongue to a boil over high heat, then cover the casserole with a double thickness of aluminum foil and set its lid in place. Bake the tongue in the middle of the oven for 2½ to 3 hours, or until it shows no resistance when pierced deeply with a fork.

If you plan to serve the tongue hot, transfer it to a heated platter. Skim and discard as much fat as possible from the surface of the cooking liquid, then strain the liquid through a fine sieve into a small bowl. Taste for seasoning, and present the sauce in a sauceboat with the tongue.

If you plan to serve the tongue cold, let it cool to room temperature in the cooking liquid; refrigerate until ready to serve. Transfer the tongue to a platter or cutting board, trim it and carve it into thin slices. Arrange the slices on a chilled platter. Skim and strain the cooking liquid as described above and serve it with the tongue. Mobile thyme tongue is frequently accompanied by pickled watermelon rind (*Recipe Index*).

Country Ham Stuffed with Greens

A 12- to 16-pound country ham
3 tablespoons butter
¼ cup finely chopped scallions,
 including 2 inches of the green
 tops
½ cup finely chopped celery
½ pound fresh mustard greens,
 trimmed, washed and coarsely
chopped (about 4 cups)
½ pound fresh spinach, trimmed,
 washed and coarsely chopped
 (about 4 cups)
1 teaspoon crushed dried hot red
 pepper
½ teaspoon salt
Freshly ground black pepper

Starting a day ahead, place the ham in a pot large enough to hold it comfortably and pour in enough cold water to cover the ham by at least 1 inch. Let the ham soak at room temperature for at least 12 hours.

When you are ready to cook the ham drain off the soaking water and replace it with fresh cold water to cover the ham by 1 inch. Bring to a boil over high heat, then reduce the heat to low and simmer the ham partially covered for 1 hour. Transfer the ham to cool on a large platter or cutting board. Discard the cooking liquid, wash the pot and set it aside.

With a large sharp knife, cut the rind off the ham and discard it. Then remove the excess fat from the entire outside surface of the ham, leaving a layer no more than ⅛ inch thick all around. Set the ham aside.

In a heavy 4- to 5-quart saucepan, melt the butter over moderate heat. When the foam begins to subside, add the scallions and celery and, stirring frequently, cook for about 5 minutes until they are soft and transparent but not brown. Stir in the mustard greens, spinach, red pepper, salt and a few grindings of black pepper. Reduce the heat to the lowest possible setting, cover the pan tightly, and cook for 15 minutes, or until all the vegetables are tender.

Following the directions opposite, cut 6 to 8 incisions in the ham and stuff them with the mustard-green-and-spinach mixture. Wrap the ham, as shown, in cheesecloth.

Return the ham to the original pot and add enough water to cover by at least 1 inch. Bring to a boil over high heat, reduce the heat to low and partially cover the pot. Simmer for 3 to 4 hours, allowing about 15 minutes to the pound, or until the ham is tender and shows no resistance when pierced deeply with the point of a small skewer or sharp knife. (The ham should be kept constantly immersed in water. Check the pot from time to time and add more boiling water if necessary.) The cooking liquid can be saved, if you like, for cooking greens.

Transfer the ham to a large platter and, without removing the cheesecloth, cool to room temperature and refrigerate for at least 12 hours. Just before serving, unwrap the ham and with a large sharp knife, carve it into paper-thin slices as shown opposite.

TO STUFF A COUNTRY HAM WITH GREENS: (1) Cut off and discard the rind and most of the fat. (2) Make 6 to 8 deep incisions in the ham, each about 2 inches long and spaced about 2 inches apart. (3) Holding the incisions apart with a spoon, fill them evenly with the greens. (4) Wrap the stuffed ham in a double thickness of cheesecloth. (5) Sew up the ends of the cheesecloth with kitchen cord. Following the recipe opposite, cook, cool and chill the wrapped ham. (6) Carve horizontally into paper-thin slices.

53

Chitterlings

To serve 8 to 10

2 cups distilled white vinegar
1 pound salt
10 pounds chitterlings (hog entrails)
2 hog maws
2 cups coarsely chopped onions
2 fresh hot red chilies, each about 3 inches long, washed, stemmed

and coarsely chopped (*caution: see note, page 3*)
1½ cups coarsely chopped celery
1 teaspoon freshly ground black pepper
1 green pepper, cut in half lengthwise, stemmed, seeded and coarsely chopped
3 cups water

Fill a large basin with cold water and stir in the vinegar and salt. Drop in the chitterlings and hog maws, and soak undisturbed for 30 minutes. Drain off the water, peel off and discard the fat from the chitterlings and hog maws, and rinse the meats under cold running water. Soak the chitterlings and hog maws in fresh cold water for 1 to 2 hours longer, changing the water several times. Rinse the meats again under cold running water and place them in an 8- to 10-quart casserole. Add the onions, chilies, celery, black pepper, green pepper and 3 cups of water, and bring to a boil over high heat. Cover the casserole tightly, reduce the heat to low, and simmer for about 3 hours, or until almost all of the liquid has evaporated and the chitterlings and hog maws are tender. Serve at once, accompanied by potato salad, boiled greens and cornbread (*Recipe Index*) and by a cruet of vinegar.

If you prefer the chitterlings fried, prepare and boil them as described above. Pat them thoroughly dry with paper towels and place them in an ungreased heavy 10- to 12-inch skillet, preferably one with a nonstick surface. Fry uncovered over moderately high heat, turning them frequently with tongs or a wooden spoon until they are golden brown.

Ham Hocks and Greens

To serve 4 to 6

2 pounds ham hocks
¼ pound salt pork (with rind removed), cut into ½-inch pieces
1 cup coarsely chopped onions
1 fresh hot red chili, about 3 inches long, washed, stemmed, seeded

and coarsely chopped (*caution: see note, page 3*)
1 teaspoon sugar
2 bunches collard, turnip or mustard greens, stripped from their stems and thoroughly washed (about 12 cups)

Place the ham hocks in a heavy 4- to 6-quart casserole and add enough water to cover the meat by at least 1 inch. Bring to a boil over moderate heat, then lower the heat and simmer uncovered for 2 hours. Check the water from time to time and add more if it evaporates too quickly.

Meanwhile, drop the salt pork pieces into a pot of boiling water and boil for about 3 minutes. Drain them immediately and pat them dry with paper towels. Then drop the salt pork into a 10- to 12-inch skillet and fry over moderate heat for 8 to 10 minutes, turning the pieces frequently with a wooden spoon, until they are crisp and brown and have rendered all their fat. Remove the skillet from the heat and set aside.

When the ham hocks have cooked their allotted time, stir in the salt pork and its fat, the onions, chili, sugar and greens. Cover the casserole tightly, reduce the heat to low, and simmer for 45 minutes. Taste for seasoning. With a slotted spoon, transfer the greens to a large heated platter and place the ham hocks on top. Serve with cornbread and a bowl of the "pot likker" from the casserole as a dunking sauce for the bread.

Ham Hocks and Black-eyed Peas

To serve 6 to 8

2 one-pound smoked ham hocks, or substitute a meaty ham bone or pieces of slab bacon with the rind on
2 cups (1 pound) dried black-eyed peas
1 cup coarsely chopped onions
2 medium-sized celery stalks,
trimmed of all leaves and coarsely chopped
1 fresh hot red chili, about 3 inches long, washed, stemmed, seeded if desired, and coarsely chopped
(caution: see note, page 3)
Freshly ground black pepper

Place the ham hocks in a heavy 4- to 6-quart pot and add enough water to cover the meat by at least 1 inch. Bring to a boil over high heat, reduce the heat to low and simmer partially covered for 2 hours, or until the ham hocks are tender and show no resistance when pierced deeply with the point of a small skewer or sharp knife.

In a sieve or colander, wash the black-eyed peas under cold running water until the draining water is clear. Add the peas, onions, celery, chili and a few grindings of black pepper to the pot, mix well, and bring to a boil over high heat. Reduce the heat to low and simmer partially covered for 1 to 1½ hours, or until the peas are tender. Check the pot from time to time and add more boiling water if necessary. When the peas are fully cooked, they should have absorbed almost all of the pan liquid.

Taste for seasoning and serve at once from a heated platter or bowl.

Ham Mousse

To serve 8

2 teaspoons vegetable oil
2 envelopes unflavored gelatin
¼ cup dry sherry
1⅓ cups chicken stock, freshly
    made or canned

2 eggs, separated
3½ cups cooked ground
    Smithfield or country ham
    *(leftover from baked ham, pages
    52 and 61)*
1 cup heavy cream

Brush a 1-quart mold with the oil and invert it on a paper towel to let the excess oil drain off. Soften the gelatin in the sherry for about 5 minutes.

Meanwhile, pour the chicken stock into a 1- to 1½-quart enameled or stainless-steel saucepan. Bring to a boil over high heat, then lower the heat so that the stock barely simmers. Beat the egg yolks lightly in a small bowl and gradually beat in ¼ cup of the hot stock. Then pour the mixture into the simmering stock, beating constantly with a wire whisk. Add the gelatin mixture and simmer over low heat for a minute or two, stirring constantly, until the gelatin has completely dissolved. Stir in the ground ham and remove the pan from the heat.

With a wire whisk or a rotary or electric beater, beat the egg whites until they are firm enough to form unwavering peaks on the beater when it is lifted from the bowl. In a separate bowl and with a clean beater, whip the cream until it holds soft peaks on the beater. Fold the whipped cream and egg whites into the gelatin mixture, continuing to fold until streaks of white no longer show. Pour the mousse into the prepared mold, smooth the top with a spatula, and refrigerate for at least 2 hours, until firm.

To unmold the mousse, run a small knife around the inside edge of the mold and dip the bottom of the mold briefly in hot water. Place a chilled platter on top of the mold, invert, and rap it once or twice on the table. The mousse should slide out easily. Serve at once, or refrigerate for up to 3 or 4 hours.

Ham with Red-Eye Gravy

To serve 4

4 slices country ham, cut ¼ inch thick   1 cup freshly brewed coffee

With a sharp knife, trim the excess fat from the ham slices and cut the fat into small bits. Place the fat in a heavy ungreased 12-inch skillet and, stirring frequently, fry over moderate heat until the bits are crisp and have rendered all their fat.

Remove and discard the bits of fat and in their place add the ham slices. Fry the ham in the rendered fat, turning the slices with tongs or a wide metal spatula and regulating the heat so that they color richly and evenly without burning.

Transfer the fried ham to a heated platter and pour the coffee into the skillet. Bring to a boil over high heat, meanwhile scraping in the brown bits that cling to the bottom of the pan. Boil briskly, uncovered, until the gravy turns red, then pour it over the ham and serve at once.

Ham with red-eye gravy is a favorite breakfast dish, traditionally accompanied by boiled grits or hot biscuits—or both.

Homesteaders' Ham Loaf

To serve 6 to 8

HAM LOAF	
1 tablespoon vegetable oil	½ pound ground lean fresh pork
1 pound (about 3 cups) ground cooked country ham *(leftover from baked ham, pages 52 and 61)*	1 cup dry bread crumbs
	2 tablespoons prepared mustard
	1 egg, lightly beaten
	½ cup grated onions
	½ cup milk

Preheat the oven to 350°. With a pastry brush, spread the tablespoon of oil evenly over the bottom of a shallow roasting pan. Set aside.

In a large mixing bowl, combine the ground ham, fresh pork, bread crumbs, prepared mustard, egg, onions and milk. Knead briefly with your hands to mix the ingredients thoroughly, then transfer the mixture to the roasting pan and pat and shape it into a loaf about 8 inches long, 4 inches wide and 3 inches high.

SAUCE	
¼ cup dark brown sugar	2 tablespoons cold water
½ teaspoon dry mustard	2 tablespoons distilled white vinegar

To make the sauce, beat the sugar, dry mustard, water and vinegar together in a small mixing bowl. Spoon 2 tablespoons of the sauce over the ham loaf, then place the loaf in the middle of the oven and bake for 1 hour, basting every 10 minutes or so until you have used all the remaining sauce.

Serve the ham loaf at once, from a heated platter. Or, if you prefer the ham loaf cold, let it cool to room temperature, cover with foil or plastic wrap, and refrigerate for several hours.

Set a precooked ham on an 18-inch square of pastry dough and fold two ends of the dough over the sides of the ham. Holding the dough firmly in place, turn the ham over.

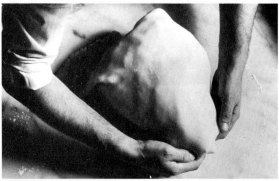

Gently fold the dough under and around the entire ham, following its shape. Be careful not to tear the dough.

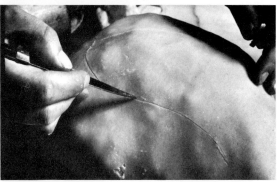

To decorate the ham as shown opposite, sketch the outline of the stems in the dough with a knife point.

Roll out the remaining dough and, with a cookie cutter or small knife, cut out pastry leaves. Lift up the leaves with the knife.

With the edge of the knife, firmly delineate the veins of a leaf. Then brush the bottoms of the leaves with an egg-and-cream mixture.

Set the leaves along the stem outlines on the ham, overlapping them slightly.

To make roses, roll up 3-by-1-inch strips of dough. Pull the outer flap down slightly while pushing up the center, and trim off ½ inch from the bottom of the rose. Brush the flowers and ham *(below)* with the egg-and-cream mixture and bake *(page 60)*.

Baked Ham in Pastry

6 egg yolks
½ to 1 cup ice water
A 12- to 14-pound precooked ham
1 egg yolk, lightly beaten and
combined with 3 tablespoons
heavy cream

6 cups flour
12 tablespoons butter, chilled and
cut into ¼-inch bits
12 tablespoons lard, chilled and cut
into ¼-inch bits

In a large chilled mixing bowl, combine the flour, butter and lard. With your fingertips rub the flour and fat together until they look like coarse meal. Mix the egg yolks thoroughly into the dough. Pour ½ cup of the ice water over the mixture all at once, knead vigorously and gather the dough into a ball. If the dough crumbles, add up to ½ cup more ice water, a tablespoonful at a time, until the particles adhere. Dust the dough with a little flour, wrap it in wax paper and refrigerate one hour.

Preheat the oven to 350°. Cut off about ¼ of the dough and return it to the refrigerator. Place the remaining dough on a lightly floured surface and pat it into a rough square about 1 inch thick. Then roll the dough into approximately an 18-inch square.

Pat the ham completely dry with paper towels and, following the directions on page 78, enclose it securely in the square of dough. Place the covered ham on a large ungreased baking sheet and set aside.

On the lightly floured surface, roll the reserved ¼ of the dough into a rough circle ⅛ inch thick. With pastry cutters or a sharp knife, cut out leaves, crescents and other decorations like those in the photograph on page 78. With a pastry brush, moisten the bottom of each decoration lightly with the egg-yolk-and-cream mixture and set each decoration in place on the ham as illustrated on page 78. Finally, brush the entire surface of the ham with the remaining egg-yolk-and-cream mixture. Bake in the middle of the oven for 1 hour, or until the crust is golden brown.

To serve, transfer the ham to a heated platter. Let the ham cool to room temperature before carving it into ½-inch-thick slices.

Baked Ham with Brown-Sugar Glaze

In the South, Smithfield and other types of country ham are never served as a main meat course; instead, paper-thin slivers of the smoked, salty hams are presented as a first course or as an accompaniment to chicken or other fowl. They are also a traditional part of buffet tables. All of these hams are available baked and ready to serve—but at a higher price than the uncooked ones command. If you would like to prepare your own ham, the following recipe describes the basic procedures.

A 12- to 16-pound Smithfield ham or a 12- to 16-pound Virginia, Kentucky, Tennessee or Georgia country ham

½ to ¾ cup fine dry bread crumbs
1 cup dark brown sugar
¼ cup whole cloves (optional)

Starting a day ahead, place the ham in a pot large enough to hold it comfortably and pour in enough water to cover the ham by at least 1 inch. Let the ham soak for at least 12 hours (for 24 hours if possible), changing the water 2 or 3 times. Remove the ham from the pot and discard the soaking water. Then, under lukewarm running water, scrub the ham vigorously with a stiff brush to remove any traces of pepper or mold.

With a dampened kitchen towel wipe the ham and return it to the pot. Pour in enough water to cover the ham by at least 1 inch and bring to a simmer over high heat. Reduce the heat to low and simmer partially covered for 3 to 4 hours, allowing 15 to 20 minutes to the pound. When the ham is fully cooked, you should be able to move and easily pull out the small bone near the shank.

Transfer the ham to a platter and, if you wish, set the cooking water aside to be used for cooking greens. When the ham is cool enough to handle remove the rind with a small sharp knife, leaving only a ⅛-inch-thick layer of fat. If you intend to stud the ham with cloves, make crisscrossing cuts about 1 inch apart on the fatty side, slicing down through the fat to the meat.

Preheat the oven to 400°. With your fingers, press enough of the bread crumbs into the fatty side of the ham to coat it thoroughly. Then sift the brown sugar evenly over the crumbs. If you are using cloves, insert them where the scoring lines intersect. Place the ham on a rack set in a shallow roasting pan and bake it uncovered in the middle of the oven for about 20 minutes, or until the glaze is richly browned.

Set the ham on a large platter and let it cool to room temperature before serving. Smithfield or country ham is carved into paper-thin slices as shown opposite. Tightly covered with foil or plastic wrap, the ham can safely be kept in the refrigerator for at least 1 month.

SALADS

Fat Salad

To serve 4

½ pound snap beans, washed,
    trimmed and cut in half crosswise
    (2 cups)
1 small head romaine lettuce
2 tablespoons finely chopped parsley
2 tablespoons finely cut chives

¼ cup thinly sliced Bermuda onion
½ teaspoon salt
Freshly ground black pepper
¼ pound fatback, finely chopped
    (½ cup)
½ cup distilled white vinegar

Place the beans in enough boiling water to cover them by 1 inch. Cook uncovered over moderate heat for about 8 to 10 minutes, or until the beans are tender but still slightly crisp to the bite. Drain at once in a colander and wash the beans under cold running water. Set aside to cool to room temperature, then spread them out on paper towels and pat thoroughly dry with another towel.

Separate the lettuce and wash the leaves under cold running water. Dry each leaf thoroughly with paper towels, then cut the leaves into serving-sized pieces and scatter them in the bottom of a glass or porcelain salad bowl. Add the beans, parsley, chives, onions, salt and several grindings of pepper, and toss together with two large spoons—or with your hands if you like.

Place the chopped fatback in an 8- to 10-inch skillet and fry over moderately high heat until it has rendered all of its fat and the bits are crisp and brown. Remove the pan from the heat and stir in the vinegar, then pour the contents of the skillet over the salad. Toss once more, taste for seasoning and serve at once.

Coleslaw with Boiled Dressing

To serve 8 to 10

½ cup cider vinegar
⅓ cup water
2 tablespoons sugar
2 tablespoons flour
2 teaspoons dry mustard

2 teaspoons salt
½ cup heavy cream
2 tablespoons butter
4 eggs, lightly beaten
2 pounds firm white cabbage
1 cup grated scraped carrots

In a 2- to 3-quart saucepan, combine the vinegar, water, sugar, flour, mustard and salt and beat vigorously with a wire whisk until the mixture is smooth. Place over moderate heat and, whisking constantly, add the cream and butter and cook until the butter melts and the sauce comes to a simmer. Stir 2 or 3 tablespoonfuls of the simmering liquid into the beaten eggs and, when they are well incorporated, pour the mixture into the sauce, whisking it constantly. Reduce the heat to low and continue to whisk until the sauce thickens heavily. With a rubber spatula, scrape the contents of the saucepan into a deep bowl and cool to room temperature.

Wash the head of cabbage under cold running water, remove the tough outer leaves, and cut the cabbage into quarters. To shred the cabbage, cut out the core and slice the quarters crosswise into ⅛-inch-wide strips.

Add the shredded cabbage and the carrots to the sauce, toss together gently but thoroughly and taste for seasoning. Cover with foil or plastic wrap and refrigerate for 2 or 3 hours before serving.

Country-Style Potato Salad

To serve 6 to 8

3 pounds large boiling potatoes,
    scrubbed under cold water and
    left unpeeled
½ cup cider vinegar
1 cup finely diced celery
1 cup finely diced onions

½ cup finely diced green pepper
½ cup finely diced sweet mixed pickles
A pinch of ground cinnamon
2 teaspoons salt
⅛ teaspoon freshly ground black
    pepper
2 cups mayonnaise, freshly made
    (page 75) or bottled

Drop the potatoes into enough boiling salted water to cover them by 1 inch. Cook uncovered over moderate heat until they are tender and offer only the slightest resistance when pierced deeply with a knife. Drain the potatoes in a colander and, as soon as they are cool enough to handle, peel and cut them into ½-inch dice. Transfer the dice to a large bowl, add the cider vinegar, and toss together gently but thoroughly with a rubber spatula.

Continued on next page   63

In a separate mixing bowl, combine the celery, onions, green pepper, pickles, cinnamon, salt, pepper and mayonnaise. Add the diced potatoes and toss gently with the spatula. Taste for seasoning, then cover with plastic wrap or foil and set aside at room temperature for at least 3 hours before serving.

Southern Chicken Salad with Boiled Dressing

To serve 6 to 8

CHICKEN SALAD

Two 3- to 3½-pound chickens, each cut into 6 to 8 pieces
1 small onion, peeled and cut into ¼-inch-thick slices
1 medium-sized carrot, scraped and cut into ¼-inch-thick slices
½ cup coarsely chopped celery leaves

3 sprigs fresh parsley
2 tablespoons salt
10 whole black peppercorns
4 hard-cooked eggs, finely chopped
1 cup finely chopped celery
½ cup finely chopped scallions, including 3 inches of the green tops
¼ cup strained fresh lemon juice

Combine the chicken, onion, carrot, celery leaves, parsley, 2 tablespoons of salt and the peppercorns in a heavy 4- to 5-quart casserole and pour in enough water to immerse the chicken completely. Bring to a boil over high heat, reduce the heat to low and simmer partially covered for 30 to 40 minutes, or until the chicken is tender but not falling apart.

With tongs or a slotted spoon, transfer the chicken to a platter or cutting board. (Strain the cooking liquid through a fine sieve, pressing down hard on the vegetables with the back of a spoon before discarding them. Reserve the stock for another use.) Remove the skin and bones from the chicken and discard them. Cut the meat into 1-inch pieces and place them in a serving bowl. Add the eggs, celery, scallions and lemon juice and with a wooden spoon toss together gently but thoroughly. Cover with foil or plastic wrap and refrigerate until ready to serve.

BOILED DRESSING

3 tablespoons sugar
1 tablespoon flour
1 teaspoon dry mustard
1 teaspoon salt

½ cup distilled white vinegar
½ cup water
1 tablespoon butter
2 eggs, lightly beaten

Meanwhile, prepare the boiled dressing in the following fashion: In a small enameled or stainless-steel saucepan, mix the sugar, flour, mustard and 1 teaspoon of salt together. With a wire whisk, stir in the vinegar, water and butter and cook over moderate heat, whisking constantly until the mixture comes to a boil and thickens lightly. Stir 1 or 2 tablespoonfuls of the simmering liquid into the beaten eggs, then pour the heated eggs into the saucepan and whisk until smooth. With a rubber spatula, transfer the dressing to a bowl and let it cool to room temperature.

Just before serving, pour the boiled dressing over the chicken mixture and stir until all the pieces of chicken and vegetables are evenly moistened.

White Bean Salad with Fresh Herbs and Mustard Dressing
To serve 6 to 8

1 quart water
1 cup (½ pound) dried navy or
   pea beans
2 teaspoons salt
1 tablespoon tarragon vinegar
2 teaspoons prepared mustard
2 drops Tabasco
¼ teaspoon freshly ground black
   pepper
⅓ cup olive oil

2 tablespoons finely cut fresh basil
2 tablespoons finely cut fresh chives
2 tablespoons finely chopped fresh
   parsley
1 teaspoon finely cut fresh dill
3 small mint leaves, finely cut
½ teaspoon finely chopped garlic
2 medium-sized firm ripe tomatoes,
   peeled, seeded and coarsely
   chopped *(see shrimp pilau, page
   29)*

In a heavy 2- to 3-quart saucepan, bring the water to a boil over high heat. Drop in the dried beans and boil them uncovered for about 2 minutes. Turn off the heat and let the beans soak uncovered for 1 hour. Then add ½ teaspoon of the salt and bring to a boil again. Reduce the heat to low, partially cover the pan and simmer for about 1 hour, or until the beans are tender but still intact. Drain the beans and set them aside in a bowl to cool to room temperature.

Combine the vinegar, mustard, Tabasco, the remaining 1½ teaspoons of salt and the pepper in a small bowl and, with a wire whisk, stir them to a smooth paste. Whisking the mixture constantly, pour in the oil in a slow stream and continue to beat until the dressing is thick and creamy.

Place the basil, chives, parsley, dill, mint and garlic in a large serving bowl and mix them well. Add the cooled beans and the tomatoes, stir gently together, then pour in the mustard dressing. Stir gently again until the beans and tomatoes are thoroughly coated with the herbs and dressing.

Cover tightly with foil or plastic wrap and marinate in the refrigerator for at least 4 hours. Just before serving, taste for seasoning and stir the salad briefly.

VEGETABLES & GRAINS

Braised Celery with Almonds

To serve 6 to 8

2 bunches celery
4 sprigs parsley
1 small bay leaf
2 cups chicken stock, freshly made
   or canned

1 teaspoon salt
⅛ teaspoon white pepper
3 tablespoons butter
3 tablespoons flour
½ cup heavy cream
¼ cup toasted slivered almonds

Remove the green leaves from the celery, bunch them together with the parsley and bay leaf, and tie them into a bouquet with string. Cut the celery ribs in half lengthwise, then slice crosswise into 1-inch lengths. Wash the pieces under cold running water, drain and drop them into a 2- to 3-quart saucepan. Pour in the chicken stock, add the bouquet, salt and pepper, and bring to a boil over high heat. Cover the pan, reduce the heat to low, and simmer for 15 minutes, until the celery is tender but still slightly resistant to the bite. With a slotted spoon, transfer the celery to a heated platter and drape with aluminum foil to keep it warm while you make the sauce.

Pour the contents of the pan through a fine sieve. Discard the herb bouquet and all but 1 cup of the cooking liquid.

In a 1- to 1½-quart saucepan, melt the butter over moderate heat. Stir in the flour, and mix together thoroughly. Stirring the mixture constantly with a wire whisk, pour in the cream and the reserved cup of cooking liquid in a slow, thin stream. Cook over high heat until the sauce comes to a boil and thickens heavily. Reduce the heat and simmer 3 minutes longer, to remove any raw taste of flour. Taste for seasoning, and pour over the celery. Scatter the almonds on top and serve at once.

Kentucky Minted Carrots

To serve 4

1 pound (about 8 to 10) medium-
 sized carrots, trimmed, washed,
 scraped and cut diagonally into
 ¼-inch lengths
1 cup water

1 teaspoon salt
3 tablespoons unsalted butter, cut
 into bits
Freshly ground black pepper
2 tablespoons coarsely cut fresh
 mint leaves

Place the carrots in a 1-quart saucepan and add the water and salt. Cover the pan tightly and bring to a boil over high heat, then reduce the heat to moderate and cook the carrots for about 15 minutes, or until the water is almost completely evaporated and the carrots are tender but still slightly resistant to the bite. Stir in the butter and several grindings of pepper, then remove the pan from the heat. Toss the carrots lightly with the mint, taste for seasoning and serve at once, in a heated vegetable dish.

Plantation String Beans

To serve 4

4 slices lean bacon, cut into
 ½-inch dice
½ cup thinly sliced scallion rounds
1 pound green beans, washed and
 trimmed
1 tablespoon cold water

1 teaspoon salt
¼ teaspoon freshly ground black
 pepper
1½ teaspoons red wine vinegar
2 tablespoons finely cut fresh mint
 leaves (optional)

Fry the bacon dice in a 10- to 12-inch enameled or stainless-steel skillet, turning them frequently with a wooden spoon until they are brown and crisp and have rendered all their fat. With a slotted spoon, transfer the dice to paper towels to drain.

Drop the scallions into the fat and, stirring occasionally, cook over moderate heat for 3 to 4 minutes, until they are soft but not brown. Now add the beans, stirring them about until they glisten with the fat. Add the tablespoon of water and cover the pan tightly. Cook over low heat for 5 minutes, then uncover the pan and continue to cook until the beans are tender but still slightly resistant to the bite. Sprinkle with the salt and pepper, stir in the vinegar, and remove from the heat. Serve from a heated dish, garnished with the bacon bits and, if you like, with the cut mint leaves.

Boiled Greens

To serve 6

3 pounds fresh young turnip,
  collard or mustard greens
1½ pounds salt pork, with rind
  removed, cut into 1-inch dice

1½ cups water
1 cup coarsely chopped onions
1 teaspoon sugar
Salt
Freshly ground black pepper

With a sharp knife trim away any bruised or blemished spots on the greens and strip the leaves from their stems. Wash the leaves in several changes of cold running water to remove all traces of dirt or sand.

In a heavy 10- to 12-inch skillet, fry the salt pork over moderate heat, stirring the dice frequently with a slotted spoon until they are crisp and brown and have rendered all their fat. Transfer the dice and liquid fat to a bowl and pour the water into the skillet. Bring to a boil over high heat, meanwhile scraping in any brown particles that cling to the bottom and sides of the pan. Remove from the heat and set aside.

Place the greens in a heavy 4- to 6-quart pot and set over high heat. Cover tightly and cook for 3 to 4 minutes, or until the greens begin to wilt. Stir in the pork fat and dice, the skillet liquid, and the onions and sugar. Cover the pot again and continue to cook over moderate heat for about 45 minutes, or until the greens are tender.

Drain off the cooking liquid and reserve it as "pot likker" for soups, or as a dunking sauce for cornbread. Taste the boiled greens, season them with as much salt and pepper as you think they need and serve at once.

Sweet Potatoes in Orange Baskets

To serve 4

4 large navel oranges
2 tablespoons unsalted butter,
  softened, plus 2 teaspoons
  unsalted butter, cut into bits
4 large sweet potatoes, boiled,
  peeled and mashed (1½ cups)

1 egg
4 teaspoons salt
½ teaspoon white pepper
¼ teaspoon grated lemon rind
2 tablespoons finely chopped
  walnuts

Preheat the oven to 350°. With a sharp heavy knife, cut off and discard a 1-inch-deep slice from the stem end of each orange. Squeeze the oranges and use the juice for some other purpose. With a small sharp knife, scrape and cut away the pulp and membranes from the orange shells, keeping the shells intact and as regular in shape as possible. Set the shells side by side in a baking dish just large enough to hold them.

In a large mixing bowl, beat the softened butter into the mashed sweet potatoes, then beat in the egg, salt, white pepper and lemon rind. Taste for seasoning. Fill each orange basket with the potato mixture, swirling the tops attractively with a rubber spatula. Sprinkle the filling with the walnuts, and dot with the butter bits, dividing the bits equally among the baskets. Bake in the center of the oven for 45 minutes, until the tops are lightly browned. Serve at once, with roast ham or chicken.

Candied Sweet Potatoes

To serve 6 to 8

1 cup sugar
¼ cup strained fresh orange juice
½ teaspoon ground cinnamon
½ teaspoon ground nutmeg
4 large sweet potatoes (about
    3 pounds), peeled, cut in half
    lengthwise, then cut into
    ½-inch-thick lengths
1 lemon, thinly sliced
8 tablespoons (1 quarter-pound
    stick) unsalted butter, cut into
    bits

Preheat the oven to 350°. In a small mixing bowl, combine the sugar, orange juice, cinnamon and nutmeg. Arrange the sweet potatoes in layers in a baking dish about 15 inches long, 10 inches wide and 2 inches high, moistening each layer with the sugar mixture and a scattering of lemon slices and butter bits. Top with the remaining butter bits and bake uncovered in the center of the oven for 1¼ hours, basting the potatoes with the liquid in the dish halfway through the cooking time.

When the potatoes can be easily pierced with the tip of a knife, serve at once, directly from the dish or on a heated platter.

Summertime Vegetable Aspic

To serve 4 to 6

9 medium-sized firm ripe tomatoes (about 3 pounds), washed, cored and coarsely chopped
2 medium-sized onions, peeled and coarsely chopped
½ cup coarsely chopped celery leaves
2 fresh parsley sprigs
1 small bay leaf
½ cup cold water
4 teaspoons unflavored gelatin
1 tablespoon strained fresh lemon juice
2 teaspoons salt
Freshly ground black pepper
1 cup finely shredded cabbage
½ cup coarsely chopped celery
⅓ cup finely chopped green pepper
1 medium-sized carrot, scraped and cut crosswise into ⅛-inch-thick slices
2 tablespoons finely chopped fresh parsley
1 tablespoon finely chopped pimiento

Combine the tomatoes, onions, celery leaves, parsley sprigs, bay leaf and ¼ cup of cold water in a 3- to 4-quart enameled or stainless-steel saucepan and bring to a boil over high heat, stirring from time to time. Reduce the heat to low and simmer partially covered for 30 minutes, or until the vegetables are very soft. Strain the contents of the pan through a fine sieve set over a bowl, pressing down on the vegetables and herbs with the back of a spoon to extract their juices before discarding them.

Meanwhile, pour the remaining ¼ cup of cold water into a small heatproof bowl and sprinkle the gelatin over it. When the gelatin has softened for 2 or 3 minutes, set the bowl in a skillet of simmering water and cook over low heat, stirring constantly, until the gelatin dissolves completely.

Stir the dissolved gelatin into the vegetable juices, add the lemon juice, salt and a few grindings of black pepper, and taste for seasoning. Refrigerate until the mixture begins to thicken and is syrupy. Then stir in the cabbage, celery, green pepper, carrot, parsley and pimiento.

Rinse a 3-cup mold under cold running water and invert it to drain. Pour the vegetable aspic mixture into the mold, cover with foil or plastic wrap and refrigerate for at least 4 hours, or until firm to the touch.

To unmold and serve the aspic, run a thin-bladed knife around the edges of the mold to loosen the sides and dip the bottom briefly in hot water. Place an inverted serving plate over the mold and, grasping plate and mold together firmly, turn them over. Rap the plate sharply on a table and the vegetable aspic should slide out easily.

Hopping John

To serve 8 to 10

Hopping John is a traditional New Year's Day dish in the South. Legend holds that it must be eaten before noon on New Year's Day to ensure good luck in the coming year.

2 cups (1 pound) dried black-eyed
    peas
6 cups cold water
1 pound salt pork (rind removed),
    cut into strips about 2 inches long
and ½ inch wide
1 cup finely chopped onions
2½ cups uncooked long-grain
    white rice, not the converted
    variety

Place the black-eyed peas in a sieve or colander and run cold water over them until the draining water is clear. Transfer the peas to a 3- to 4-quart casserole, add 6 cups of cold water, and bring to a boil over high heat. Then lower the heat and simmer, partially covered, for 30 minutes.

Meanwhile, drop the salt pork strips into a pot of boiling water and bring the water back to a boil. Immediately drain the strips, pat them dry with paper towels, then place them in a 10- to 12-inch skillet. Fry uncovered over moderately high heat for 10 to 12 minutes, turning the strips frequently with a large spoon and adjusting the heat if necessary to prevent the pork from burning. When the strips are brown and crisp and have rendered all their fat, transfer them with tongs to paper towels to drain, and set aside.

Add the chopped onions to the fat remaining in the skillet and cook over moderate heat for 3 to 5 minutes, stirring frequently, until the onions are soft but not yet browned. Remove from the heat and set aside.

In a fine sieve, wash the rice under cold running water until the draining water is clear.

After the peas have cooked their allotted time, stir in the salt pork, onions and the rice and brink back to a boil. Cover the casserole tightly, reduce the heat to low, and simmer 20 to 30 minutes, or until the peas are tender and the rice is dry and fluffy. Taste for seasoning and serve at once.

Jefferson Rice

PILAU WITH PINE NUTS AND PISTACHIOS

Pilau, which originated in the Orient, was introduced to the United States by early traders. Variations of this rice dish are especially popular in the Carolinas. The following version was a favorite of Thomas Jefferson.

To serve 4 to 6

1 cup uncooked long-grain white rice, not the converted variety	4 tablespoons butter
	1 teaspoon salt
2 cups chicken stock, fresh or canned, or 2 cups water, or a combination of the two	½ cup pine nuts
	¼ cup unsalted shelled pistachios
	¼ teaspoon ground mace

Place the rice in a sieve or colander and wash it under cold running water until the draining water runs clear.

In a heavy 1- to 2-quart saucepan, bring the chicken stock or water, 1 tablespoon of the butter and ½ teaspoon of the salt to a boil over high heat. Pour in the rice, stir well, and reduce the heat to low. Cover the pan tightly and simmer for about 20 minutes, or until the rice is tender and the grains have absorbed all the liquid.

Meanwhile, in a heavy 8- to 10-inch skillet, melt the remaining 3 tablespoons of butter over moderate heat. When the foam begins to subside, add the nuts and, stirring frequently, fry until they are a delicate golden color. Remove the skillet from the heat.

Transfer the rice to a heated serving bowl and fluff it with a table fork. Then, with a rubber spatula, scrape the contents of the skillet over the rice and toss the rice and nuts gently together. Sprinkle the pilau with the mace and remaining ½ teaspoon of salt and serve at once.

Southern Dry Rice

To serve 4

	2 tablespoons unsalted butter
1 cup uncooked long-grain white rice, not the converted variety	1 teaspoon strained fresh lemon juice
1½ cups cold water	1 teaspoon salt

Place the rice in a sieve or colander and wash it under cold running water, stirring the grains with a fork until the draining water runs clear.

In a heavy 2- to 3-quart saucepan, bring the water, butter, lemon juice and salt to a boil over high heat. Pour in the rice, stir well and reduce the heat to low. Cover the pan tightly and simmer for about 20 minutes, or until the rice is tender and the grains have absorbed all the liquid. Remove the pan from the heat and, without removing the cover, set the rice aside for 10 minutes.

To serve, transfer the rice to a heated bowl and fluff it with a fork. Southern dry rice often accompanies fried chicken *(Recipe Index)*, and when it does, the chicken gravy is poured over the rice before serving.

Red Rice

To serve 4

6 slices lean bacon	1 teaspoon sugar
1 cup finely chopped onions	1 teaspoon salt
½ cup finely chopped, seeded and deribbed red bell pepper	2 medium-sized firm ripe tomatoes, peeled, seeded and coarsely
1 cup uncooked long-grain white rice, not the converted variety	chopped *(see shrimp pilau, page 29)*, or substitute 1 cup chopped
⅛ teaspoon Tabasco	drained canned tomatoes
1 teaspoon paprika	1½ cups cold water

In a heavy 10- to 12-inch skillet fry the bacon over moderate heat, turning the slices until they are crisp and brown and have rendered all their fat. Transfer to paper towels to drain, then crumble the slices coarsely.

Pour off all but about 4 tablespoons of the fat remaining in the skillet and add the onions and red pepper. Stirring frequently, cook over moderate heat for about 5 minutes, or until the onions are soft and translucent but not brown. Add the rice and stir until the grains glisten with the fat, then mix in the Tabasco, paprika, sugar, salt, tomatoes and water.

Bring to a boil over high heat, cover the skillet tightly, and reduce the heat to low. Simmer about 20 minutes, or until all of the liquid has evaporated and the rice is tender to the bite. Remove the skillet from the heat and set aside, still covered, for 10 minutes. Transfer the rice to a heated serving bowl, scatter the crumbled bacon on top, and serve at once.

Squash Cakes

To make about 3 dozen

3 to 3½ pounds (about 6 medium-sized) yellow summer squash	¼ cup milk
	½ teaspoon salt
4 tablespoons flour	1 teaspoon sugar
1 egg	Vegetable oil

With a small sharp knife, peel the squash and cut them crosswise into 2-inch chunks. Place the chunks in a large colander and set it inside a deep pot. Pour enough water into the pot to come within an inch of the bottom of the colander and bring to a boil over high heat. Cover the pot tightly, reduce the heat to low, and steam the squash for 20 minutes, or until tender but not falling apart. Purée the squash in a fine sieve set over a large mixing bowl either by mashing them with a potato masher or by forcing them through a potato ricer. With the back of a spoon, press down hard on the purée to extract as much of the liquid as possible. Discard the liquid.

Transfer the purée to a large mixing bowl and, with a wooden spoon, beat in the flour a tablespoon at a time. When it is thoroughly incorporated, beat in the egg, milk, salt and sugar. Taste for seasoning.

Pour enough oil into a heavy 10- to 12-inch skillet to come 1 inch up the sides of the pan and set it over high heat. When the fat is very hot but not yet smoking, drop in the batter by the heaping tablespoonful, flattening the mounds with the back of a spoon into 2-inch round cakes. Fry the cakes for a minute or two on each side, turning them over with a spatula. Drain the fried cakes on paper towels batch by batch as you proceed. Sprinkle the cakes liberally with salt, and serve at once.

SAUCES & DRESSINGS

Mrs. Marston's Sauce Mahonaise

MAYONNAISE

To make about 1½ cups

The yolk of 1 hard-cooked egg, cooled
2 raw egg yolks, at room temperature
½ teaspoon dry mustard
½ teaspoon salt
A pinch of ground hot red pepper (cayenne)
1 tablespoon strained fresh lemon juice or vinegar
1½ cups olive oil

Place the hard-cooked egg yolk in a large mixing bowl and mash it to a smooth paste with the back of a fork. Add the 2 raw egg yolks and, with a wire whisk or a rotary or electric beater, beat vigorously for about 2 minutes, until the yolks thicken and cling to the beater. Stir in the mustard, salt, red pepper, and lemon juice or vinegar. Beat in ½ cup of the oil, a few drops at a time; make sure each addition is absorbed before adding more. By the time ½ cup of oil has been beaten in, the mayonnaise should have the consistency of very thick cream.

Beating the mayonnaise constantly, pour in the remaining cup of oil in a slow, thin stream. Cover tightly and refrigerate until ready to use. Mayonnaise can safely be kept in the refrigerator for approximately a week.

Tomato Catsup

To make about 1 quart

12 medium-sized firm ripe tomatoes
(about 4 pounds), washed, cored
and quartered
2 cups finely chopped onions
1½ cups light brown sugar

1½ cups distilled white vinegar
5 tablespoons mixed pickling spice
1 tablespoon finely chopped fresh
hot red chili *(caution: see note,
page 3)*
1½ teaspoons salt

Combine all the ingredients in a 5- to 6-quart enameled or stainless-steel pot. Bring to a boil over high heat, stirring constantly with a wooden spoon until the brown sugar dissolves. Reduce the heat to low and simmer partially covered until the mixture is thick enough to hold its shape almost solidly in the spoon. As the catsup begins to thicken, stir from time to time (especially around the corners) to prevent it from scorching.

Rub the catsup through a fine sieve into a bowl, pressing down hard on the vegetables with the back of the spoon to extract all their juices before discarding the pulp. (Or purée the catsup through the finest blade of a food mill.) Cool to room temperature, cover with foil or plastic wrap, and chill until ready to serve. Tightly covered and refrigerated, the catsup can safely be kept for one month.

Seafood Seasoning

To make about 3 cups

3 cups coarse (kosher) salt
6 tablespoons coarsely ground black
pepper
1 tablespoon ground hot red pepper
(cayenne)

3 tablespoons dry mustard
1 tablespoon mustard seeds
1 tablespoon celery seeds
1 tablespoon ground ginger
2 teaspoons paprika

Combine all the ingredients in a deep bowl and stir until they are thoroughly mixed. Transfer the seafood seasoning to a jar, cover tightly, and store at room temperature until ready to use.

Tartar Sauce

To make about 1 cup

2 tablespoons tarragon vinegar
1 teaspoon dry mustard
⅛ teaspoon ground hot red pepper
   (cayenne)
½ teaspoon salt
¼ cup finely chopped dill pickles
2 tablespoons finely chopped onions

1 tablespoon finely cut fresh chives
1 tablespoon finely chopped fresh
   parsley
1 teaspoon finely chopped capers
1 cup freshly made mayonnaise
   (page 75), or substitute
   unsweetened bottled mayonnaise

Combine the vinegar, mustard, red pepper and salt in a bowl and beat with a wire whisk until the spices are dissolved. Stir in the pickles, onions, chives, parsley and capers. Then beat in the mayonnaise and taste for seasoning. Cover with foil or plastic wrap and refrigerate for at least 2 hours before serving.

Tartar sauce is traditionally served as an accompaniment to deep-fried soft-shell crabs or crab cakes *(Recipe Index).* Tightly covered and refrigerated, it can safely be kept for 1 or 2 days.

Monticello Salad Dressing

To make about 1 cup

1 medium-sized garlic clove, finely
   chopped
1 teaspoon salt
½ teaspoon ground white pepper,

   preferably freshly ground
⅓ cup tarragon or wine vinegar
⅓ cup domestic sesame-seed oil,
   combined with ⅓ cup olive oil

Combine the garlic, salt and white pepper in a small bowl and, with the back of a spoon, crush to a smooth paste. Beat in the vinegar by the tablespoonful. Stirring constantly with a wire whisk, pour in the sesame-and-olive-oil mixture in a slow, thin stream and continue to beat until the salad dressing is smooth.

Taste for seasoning and serve at once.

Summer Fruit Conserve

To make about 3½ quarts

16 medium-sized firm ripe peaches (about 4 pounds)	1 large orange
	3 lemons
¾ pound medium-sized firm ripe apricots	6 cups sugar
	2 cups (½ pound) seedless raisins
1 pound firm ripe cherries	2 cups (½ pound) shelled pecan halves
1 large grapefruit	1 cup bourbon

Drop the peaches and apricots into enough boiling water to cover them completely and boil briskly for 2 to 3 minutes. Drain in a sieve or colander, then remove the skins with a small sharp knife. Cut the peaches and apricots in half, discard the pits, chop the fruits coarsely and combine them in a 6- to 8-quart enameled or stainless-steel pot.

Wash, stem and pit the cherries and add them to the pot. Slice the unpeeled grapefruit, orange and lemons into ¼-inch-thick rounds and pick out the seeds with the point of a small knife. Put the slices through the coarsest blade of a food grinder and add all the pulp and juices to the peach-and-cherry mixture. Stir in the sugar, cover the pot with foil or plastic wrap and set aside at room temperature for at least 12 hours.

Stirring constantly with a wooden spoon, bring the fruit mixture to a boil over high heat. Reduce the heat to low and simmer uncovered for 1 to 1½ hours, or until the mixture is thick enough to hold its shape almost solidly in a spoon. As the conserve begins to thicken, stir deeply from time to time to prevent it from sticking to the bottom of the pot.

Add the raisins and, stirring frequently, continue to simmer for 15 minutes. Stir in the pecans and the bourbon and mix well. Immediately ladle the conserve into hot sterilized jars. Fill the jars to within ⅛ inch of the top and follow the directions for canning and sealing on page 2.

Summer fruit conserve is used as a topping for ice cream and is also served as an accompaniment to game and roast meats.

Pickled Peaches

To make about 2 quarts

12 medium-sized firm ripe peaches
 (about 3 pounds)
12 whole cloves
4½ cups sugar

3 cups cider vinegar
4 one-inch-long pieces of stick
 cinnamon, broken into bits with
 a mallet or the side of a heavy
 cleaver

Drop the peaches, 3 or 4 at a time, into a pot of boiling water and let them boil briskly for about 2 or 3 minutes. With a slotted spoon, transfer the peaches to a colander and run cold water over them. Then peel them with a small sharp knife. Pierce each peach with a whole clove and drop the peaches into wide-mouthed canning jars.

In a 2- to 3-quart enameled or stainless-steel pan, bring the sugar, vinegar and cinnamon to a boil over high heat, stirring until the sugar dissolves. Immediately ladle the hot liquid over the peaches, a few tablespoonfuls at a time, allowing the liquid and bits of cinnamon to flow through to the bottom of the jars before adding more.

Cover tightly, cool to room temperature and refrigerate for at least 3 days to let the peaches pickle before serving them. Pickled peaches are a traditional Southern accompaniment to baked ham.

Palm Beach Pineapple Relish

To make about 2 cups

A 4-pound firm ripe pineapple,
 stemmed, peeled, cored and
 coarsely chopped
2 cups sugar
1½ cups tarragon vinegar

2 two-inch pieces stick cinnamon,
 coarsely crushed with a mallet or
 the side of a cleaver and
 wrapped in cheesecloth together
 with 2 teaspoons whole cloves

Combine the pineapple, sugar, vinegar and bag of spices in a heavy 2- to 3-quart enameled casserole and bring to a boil over high heat, stirring with a wooden spoon to dissolve the sugar. Reduce the heat to moderate and, stirring from time to time, cook uncovered for about 30 minutes, or until the pineapple pieces are translucent and the mixture is thick enough to hold its shape almost solidly in the spoon. Remove and discard the cheesecloth bag of spices.

Ladle the relish immediately into hot sterilized jars, filling them to within ⅛ inch of the top and following the directions for canning and sealing on page 2. Pineapple relish is served with cold meats.

Pickled Watermelon Rind

To make about 3 quarts

A 15- to 16-pound firm ripe
    watermelon
½ cup salt
2 quarts plus 2½ quarts cold water
1¾ cups distilled white vinegar
7 cups sugar
1 teaspoon ground mace
3 one-inch-long pieces of stick

cinnamon
1 tablespoon whole allspice and
    1 tablespoon whole cloves,
    wrapped together in cheesecloth
    and tied securely
2 medium-sized lemons, cut
    crosswise into ¼-inch-thick
    slices (about 1 cup)
3 drops green food coloring

Prepare the pickled watermelon rind at least 2 weeks before you plan to serve it. With a large sharp knife, cut the watermelon crosswise in half and then cut each half lengthwise into quarters. Scrape out all the watermelon pulp with the knife or a large spoon; refrigerate the pulp for another use if you wish.

Then, with a small sharp knife or rotary vegetable peeler, cut off and discard the green skin of the watermelon, leaving only the white inner rind. Cut the rind into 1- to 1½-inch chunks and drop them into a large deep crock or enameled pot. Add the salt and 2 quarts of the water and stir until the salt dissolves. The brine should cover the rind completely; if necessary, add more water. Set the rind aside in the brine at room temperature for about 12 hours.

Pour off the brine and transfer the rind to a large colander. Rinse the chunks under cold running water, tossing them about with a spoon, until the draining water runs clear.

In an 8- to 10-quart enameled or stainless-steel pot, combine 2½ quarts of water, the vinegar, sugar, mace, cinnamon, and the wrapped allspice and cloves. Bring to a boil over high heat, stirring until the sugar dissolves. Drop in the watermelon rind and, when the mixture returns to a boil, reduce the heat to moderate. Boil gently, uncovered, for about 45 minutes, or until the rind is tender but not too soft.

Turn off the heat and pick out and discard the cheesecloth bag of spices. Add the lemon slices and food coloring to the pot and stir gently for a moment or two with a long wooden spoon.

Ladle the watermelon rind and lemon slices immediately into hot sterilized jars. Then ladle the hot liquid over the rind and lemon slices, a small amount at a time, allowing it to flow through to the bottom of the jars before adding more, and filling the jars to within ⅛ inch of the top. Follow the directions for canning and sealing, and process the jars for 5 minutes in a hot-water bath as described on page 2. Let the pickled watermelon rind stand in a cool, dark place (not the refrigerator) for at least 2 weeks before serving.

Mixed Vegetable Pickles

To make about 5 quarts

6 large firm ripe cucumbers
1 pound white cabbage, halved
  lengthwise, cored and cut into
  1-inch chunks (about 5 cups)
4 medium-sized onions, peeled and
  cut into 1-inch chunks (about
  3 cups)
2 large green bell peppers, halved
  lengthwise, seeded, deribbed
  and cut into 1-inch squares
  (about 2 cups)
1 cup salt
3 medium-sized celery ribs, trimmed
  of all leaves, halved lengthwise
and cut crosswise into 1-inch
  strips (about 2 cups)
5 medium-sized carrots, scraped and
  sliced into ⅛-inch-thick rounds
  (about 2 cups)
1 pound cauliflower, trimmed,
  washed and broken into small
  flowerets (about 3 cups)
1 pound (2 cups) dark brown sugar
¼ cup celery seeds
¼ cup mustard seeds
1 cup dry mustard
1 tablespoon turmeric
6 cups cider vinegar

With a small sharp knife, peel the cucumbers and cut them lengthwise into halves. Scoop out the seeds by running the tip of a teaspoon down the center of each half. Then cut each half lengthwise into 3 strips and slice the strips crosswise into 1-inch lengths.

Place the cucumbers, cabbage, onions and peppers in a large colander. Add the salt and toss the vegetables about with a spoon to coat them evenly. Set aside at room temperature for about 2 hours to let the excess moisture drain from the vegetables, then transfer them to a large pot or casserole. Add the celery, carrots and cauliflower, and turn the vegetables about with a spoon until they are well mixed.

In a 4- to 5-quart enameled or stainless-steel saucepan, stir the brown sugar, celery seeds, mustard seeds, dry mustard, turmeric and 1 cup of the vinegar together with a wooden spoon until the sugar and dry mustard dissolve. Stir in the remaining 5 cups of vinegar, add the vegetables and, stirring occasionally, bring to a boil over high heat. Cook briskly, uncovered, for 5 minutes.

Immediately, with a slotted spoon, transfer the vegetables to hot sterilized jars, dividing the pieces evenly among them. Ladle the hot liquid over the vegetables, a few tablespoonfuls at a time, allowing the liquid and spices to flow through to the bottom of the jars before adding more, and filling the jars to within ⅛ inch of the top. Follow the directions for canning and sealing, and process the jars 10 minutes in a hot-water bath as described on page 2.

Pear Chutney

To make about 3 pints

4 large firm green bell peppers, washed, quartered, seeded and deribbed

3 large onions (about 1½ pounds), peeled and cut into large chunks

½ cup salt

7 pounds firm pears (about 16), unpeeled but cored and cut into large chunks

2 fresh hot red chilies, about 3 inches long, washed, halved and seeded (*caution: see note, page 3*)

2 tablespoons ground turmeric

1 teaspoon celery seeds

1 teaspoon mustard seeds

6 whole allspice

4 whole cloves

2¼ cups sugar

5 cups cider vinegar

Arrange the green peppers and the onions in layers in a colander set over a deep bowl. Sprinkle each layer with salt, using ½ cup of salt in all. Drain for at least two hours, then combine the vegetables with the pears and put the mixture through the coarsest blade of a food grinder.

Wrap the chilies, turmeric, celery seeds, mustard seeds, allspice and cloves in a double thickness of cheesecloth and tie the ends securely into a bag. Combine the sugar and vinegar in a 4- to 5-quart enameled or stainless-steel casserole and bring to a boil, stirring until the sugar dissolves. Stir in the ground vegetable-and-pear mixture, drop in the cheesecloth bag and, stirring frequently with a wooden spoon, cook uncovered over moderate heat for 30 to 45 minutes, or until the mixture is thick enough to hold its shape lightly in the spoon.

Remove the pan from the heat and ladle the chutney into hot sterilized jars, filling them to within ⅛ inch of the top. Follow the directions for canning and sealing and process the jars for 5 minutes in a hot-water bath as described on page 2.

Pepper Relish

To make about 3 pints

6 large firm red bell peppers

6 large firm green bell peppers

1 fresh hot red chili, about 5 inches long (*caution: see note, page 3*)

3 large onions (about 1½ pounds), peeled and cut into chunks

2 cups distilled white vinegar

1 cup sugar

½ teaspoon mustard seeds

½ teaspoon celery seeds

Wash the red and green peppers and the chili, and pull out their stems under cold running water. Cut the peppers lengthwise into quarters, the chili into halves. Brush away the seeds with your fingers and cut out the fleshy inner ribs. Then put the peppers, chili and onions through the coarsest blade of a grinder.

Place the ground vegetables in a 4- to 5-quart enameled or stainless-steel saucepan and, with a wooden spoon, stir in the vinegar, sugar, mustard seeds and celery seeds. Bring to a boil over high heat, stirring until the sugar dissolves, and cook briskly, uncovered, for about 15 minutes, until the mixture is thick enough to hold its shape lightly in a spoon. As the relish thickens, stir frequently to keep the vegetables from scorching.

Remove the pan from the heat and ladle the relish into hot sterilized jars, filling them to within ⅛ inch of the top. Following the directions for canning and sealing, process the jars for 5 minutes in a hot-water bath as described on page 2.

Mango Chutney

To make about 3 quarts

4 pounds firm, slightly underripe mangoes, peeled, pitted and the flesh cut into 1½-inch chunks
3 cups cider vinegar
2 cups dark-brown sugar
2 cups seedless raisins
1 cup dried currants
2 cups finely chopped onions
4 large garlic cloves, peeled, finely chopped and crushed with a mortar and pestle or with the side of a cleaver or heavy knife
A 3-inch piece fresh ginger root, scraped and cut into ⅛-inch slices
1½ teaspoons ground mace
1½ teaspoons ground cloves
1 teaspoon crushed dried hot red pepper

Place the mango chunks in a 6- to 8-quart enameled or stainless-steel pot and stir in the vinegar, sugar, raisins, currants, onions, garlic, ginger root, mace, cloves and red pepper. Bring to a boil over high heat, stirring until the sugar dissolves. Then reduce the heat to low and, stirring from time to time, simmer uncovered for 30 to 40 minutes, or until the mango chunks are tender but still intact.

Ladle the chutney immediately into hot sterilized jars, filling them to within about ⅛ inch of the top and following the directions for canning and sealing on page 2.

Brandied Peaches

To make about 2 quarts

12 medium-sized firm ripe peaches (about 3 pounds)	½ cup baking soda
3 cups water	A 2-inch piece stick cinnamon
3 cups sugar	½ teaspoon ground mace
	2 cups brandy

Drop the peaches, 3 or 4 at a time, into enough boiling water to cover them completely. Boil briskly for 2 to 3 minutes, then transfer the peaches to a sieve or colander. Drain and peel them with a small sharp knife.

In a 4- to 6-quart enameled or stainless-steel pot, bring the water, sugar, baking soda, cinnamon and mace to a boil over high heat, stirring until the sugar dissolves. Add the peaches and turn them about in the liquid to moisten them evenly. Reduce the heat to low and simmer uncovered for 15 to 20 minutes, or until the peaches are tender.

With a slotted spoon, transfer the peaches to two 1-quart canning jars. Measure 2 cups of the cooking syrup into a bowl, add the brandy and mix well. Ladle the mixture over the peaches, a few tablespoonfuls at a time, allowing the liquid to flow through to the bottom of the jars before adding more. Cover tightly and set aside in a cool place (preferably not the refrigerator) for at least 3 days before serving.

Citrus Marmalade

To make about 3 pints

9 medium-sized oranges	4 lemons
1 medium-sized grapefruit	5 to 6 cups superfine sugar

Wash the oranges, grapefruit and lemons and pat them dry with paper towels. With a swivel-bladed vegetable parer, remove the peel without cutting into the bitter white pith and cut it into strips one inch long and ⅛ inch wide. Cut away the white outer pith of the fruit.

Slice the fruit in half crosswise. Wrap the halves one at a time in a double thickness of damp cheesecloth and twist the cloth to squeeze all of the juice into a bowl. Wrap all the squeezed pulp into the cloth and tie the cloth securely into a bag. Measure the juice; then add enough cold water to make 3½ quarts of liquid. Drop in the bag of pulp and the strips of peel and set aside at room temperature for at least 12 hours.

Pour the contents of the bowl—the juice and water, peel and bag of pulp—into an 8- to 10-quart enameled casserole and bring to a boil over high heat. Reduce the heat to low and, stirring frequently, simmer uncovered for 1 hour. Now measure the mixture and add 1 cup of sugar for each cup of the mixture. Bring to a boil, stirring constantly. When the sugar has dissolved, increase the heat to high and, stirring frequently, boil briskly for 20 to 30 minutes, until the marmalade reaches a temperature of 220° on a jelly, candy or deep-frying thermometer.

Remove from the heat. With a large spoon skim off the surface foam. Squeeze in the extra liquid from the pulp bag by pressing the bag against the side of the casserole with the back of a spoon. Ladle the marmalade into hot sterilized jars or jelly glasses following the instructions on page 2. To prevent the peel from floating to the top gently shake the jars occasionally as they cool.

Apple-Mint Jelly

To make about 4 cups

9 or 10 medium-sized tart cooking apples (3 pounds), about ¾ of the apples fully ripened and ¼ underripe, unpeeled but cored and coarsely chopped
3 cups water
4 to 5 cups sugar
2 tablespoons coarsely cut fresh mint leaves

Combine the apples and water in a heavy 5- to 6-quart enameled or stainless-steel saucepan and bring to a boil over high heat. Reduce the heat to low, cover tightly and simmer for 20 to 25 minutes, or until the apples are tender and can be mashed easily against the side of the pan with the back of a spoon.

Line a large colander or sieve with 4 layers of dampened cheesecloth and place it over a large enameled pot. The bottom of the colander or sieve should be suspended above the pot by at least 3 or 4 inches. Pour in the apple mixture and allow the juice to drain through undisturbed for 3 to 4 hours. (Do not squeeze the cloth or stir the juice or the finished jelly will be cloudy.)

When the juice has drained through completely, measure and return it to the enameled pot. Discard the apple pulp. Add 1 cup of sugar for each cup of juice and bring to a boil over high heat, stirring until the sugar dissolves. Cook briskly, uncovered and undisturbed, until the jelly reaches a temperature of 200° on a jelly, candy or deep-frying thermometer. Stir in the mint and continue to cook uncovered until the thermometer registers 220° (or 8° above the boiling point of water in your locality).

Remove the pot from the heat and carefully skim off the surface foam with a large spoon. Ladle the jelly into hot sterilized jars or jelly glasses, filling them to within ⅛ inch of the tops and following the directions for canning and sealing on page 2.

BREADS & BISCUITS

Spoon Bread

To serve 4 to 6

1 tablespoon butter, softened, plus
   2 tablespoons butter, cut into bits
2 cups milk
1 cup white cornmeal, preferably
   water-ground
1½ teaspoons double-acting
   baking powder
1 teaspoon salt
3 eggs, well beaten

Preheat the oven to 375°. With a pastry brush, spread the tablespoon of softened butter evenly over the bottom and sides of a 1-quart baking dish. Set aside.

In a heavy 1½- to 2-quart saucepan, heat the milk over moderate heat until bubbles begin to form around the edges of the pan. Stirring the mixture constantly with a wooden spoon, pour in the cornmeal in a slow, thin stream, stirring constantly with a wooden spoon to prevent any lumps from forming.

Remove the pan from the heat and beat in the butter bits, baking powder and salt. When the butter is completely absorbed, mix in the eggs. Then pour the batter into the baking dish and bake in the middle of the oven for about 40 minutes, or until a knife inserted in the center comes out clean. Serve the spoon bread at once, directly from its dish.

Spoon Bread with Corn

To serve 6 to 8

9 tablespoons unsalted butter, softened	water-ground
	3 egg yolks
3 medium-sized fresh ears of corn, husked	1 tablespoon sugar
	¼ teaspoon ground nutmeg, preferably freshly grated
3 cups milk	⅛ teaspoon ground hot red pepper (cayenne)
2 teaspoons salt	
1 cup white cornmeal, preferably	3 egg whites

Preheat the oven to 350°. With a pastry brush, spread 1 tablespoon of the softened butter evenly over the bottom and sides of a 2-quart casserole. Set aside.

Using the teardrop-shaped holes of a hand grater, shred the corn into a bowl. Then, with a rubber spatula, scrape the corn and the liquid that has accumulated around it into a heavy 2- to 3-quart saucepan. Add 2 cups of the milk and the salt and bring to a boil over high heat.

Pour in the cornmeal slowly enough so that the boiling continues at a rapid rate and stir constantly with a wooden spoon to keep the mixture smooth. Reduce the heat to low and, stirring from time to time, simmer uncovered until the mixture is so thick that the spoon will stand up unsupported in the middle of the pan.

Remove the pan from the heat and immediately beat in the remaining 8 tablespoons of softened butter, a few spoonfuls at a time. Add the remaining cup of milk and, when it is completely incorporated, beat in the egg yolks, one at a time, and the sugar, nutmeg and red pepper.

In a deep mixing bowl, preferably of unlined copper, beat the egg whites with a wire whisk or a rotary or electric beater until they are stiff enough to form unwavering peaks on the beater when it is lifted out of the bowl. Scoop the egg whites over the corn mixture and, with a rubber spatula, fold them together gently but thoroughly.

Pour the mixture into the buttered casserole, spreading it evenly and smoothing the top with the spatula. Bake uncovered in the center of the oven for 35 to 40 minutes, or until the top of the spoon bread is golden brown and the center barely quivers when the casserole is gently moved back and forth.

Serve the spoon bread at once, directly from the casserole.

Skillet Cornbread and Corn Sticks

To make one 9-inch bread or
fourteen 5½-inch sticks

1½ cups cornmeal, preferably
white water-ground
½ cup all-purpose flour

1 tablespoon double-acting baking
powder
1 teaspoon salt
2 eggs
1½ cups buttermilk
1 tablespoon butter, melted

Preheat the oven to 350°. Combine the cornmeal, flour, baking powder and salt and sift them into a deep bowl. In a separate bowl, beat the eggs lightly with a wire whisk or fork, then add the buttermilk and mix well. Pour the liquid ingredients over the dry ones and, with a wooden spoon, stir them together until the batter is smooth; do not overbeat.

SKILLET CORNBREAD: Place a heavy 9-inch skillet with an ovenproof handle over high heat for about 1 minute, or until the pan is very hot. Remove the pan from the heat and, with a pastry brush, quickly coat the bottom and sides of the pan with the melted butter. Immediately pour in the batter, spreading it evenly and smoothing the top with a rubber spatula. Bake in the middle of the oven for 30 to 35 minutes, or until the cornbread begins to draw away from the edges of the skillet and the top is a rich golden brown.

To unmold and serve the bread, run a knife around the edges of the pan to loosen the sides. Place a heated platter upside down over the skillet and, grasping platter and skillet together firmly, quickly invert them. Rap the platter sharply on a table and the bread should slide easily out of the skillet. Cut the bread into wedge-shaped pieces and serve at once.

CORN STICKS: Brush the inside surfaces of the molds in a corn-stick pan with the melted butter. Spoon the batter into the molds, dividing it evenly among them. Bake in the middle of the oven for 25 to 30 minutes, or until the corn sticks are golden brown.

Turn the corn sticks out of the pan, arrange them attractively on a heated platter and serve at once.

NOTE: An interesting variation on skillet cornbread is crackling bread. It may be made in the following fashion: Place ¼ pound of finely chopped salt pork or fat back in an ungreased 9-inch skillet with an ovenproof handle. Fry the pork over moderate heat, stirring frequently until the bits are crisp and brown and have rendered all their fat.

With a slotted spoon, transfer the browned pork bits (called cracklings) to paper towels to drain; then stir them into the cornbread batter. Discard all but a thin film of fat from the skillet and heat the pan until it is very hot but not smoking. Pour in the batter, spread and smooth it with a rubber spatula and bake the bread in a preheated 350° oven for 30 to 35 minutes, or until the top is golden brown. Unmold and serve the crackling bread as described in the recipe for skillet cornbread.

Sally Lunn

To make one 10-inch loaf

¼ cup lukewarm water (110° to 115°) ¾ cup lukewarm milk (110° to 115°)
1 package active dry yeast 3 eggs
1 tablespoon plus ¼ cup sugar 12 tablespoons butter, softened and
4 to 4½ cups flour cut into ½-inch bits, plus 2
2 teaspoons salt tablespoons butter, softened

Pour the lukewarm water into a small bowl and sprinkle the yeast and 1 tablespoon of the sugar over it. Let the mixture rest for 3 minutes, then mix. Set the bowl in a warm, draft-free place (such as an unlighted oven) for 10 minutes, or until the mixture almost doubles in volume.

Combine 4 cups of the flour, the remaining ¼ cup of sugar and the salt and sift them together into a deep bowl. Make a well in the center and into it pour the yeast, lukewarm milk and eggs. With a wooden spoon, gradually incorporate the dry ingredients into the liquid ones and stir until smooth. Beat in the 12 tablespoons of butter bits, a little at a time, and beat until the dough can be gathered into a compact ball. Place the dough on a lightly floured surface and knead by pushing it down with the heels of your hands, pressing it forward and folding it back on itself. As you knead, work in up to ½ cup more flour, sprinkling it over the dough and adding only enough to make a firm dough. Knead for about 15 minutes, or until the dough is smooth, shiny and elastic.

With a pastry brush, spread 1 tablespoon of softened butter over the inside of a large bowl. Drop in the dough and turn it about to butter the entire surface. Drape the bowl with a kitchen towel and place it in the draft-free place for about 30 minutes, or until it doubles in volume.

Brush the remaining tablespoon of softened butter over the bottom and sides of a 10-inch Turk's-head mold. Punch the dough down with a single blow of your fist. Then shape it into a ball and place it in the buttered mold. Drape with a towel and set aside in the draft-free place for about 1 hour, or until the loaf doubles in bulk.

Preheat the oven to 350°. Bake in the middle of the oven for 45 to 50 minutes, or until the bread is golden brown. Turn the bread out of the mold and rap the bottom with your fingertips. If it does not sound hollow, return it to the mold and bake for 5 to 10 minutes longer. Turn the bread out on a wire cake rack and serve warm or at room temperature.

NOTE: If you prefer, Sally Lunn may be baked in muffin tins. Prepare the dough as described above and let it rise once. Brush 1 tablespoon of butter evenly over the inside surfaces of 16 three-inch muffin tin cups. Then punch the dough down, divide it into 16 equal portions and shape each of these into a small ball. Place the balls in the buttered muffin cups, drape with a towel and set them aside in a draft-free place for about 45

Continued on next page

minutes, or until they double in bulk. Bake in the middle of a preheated 350° oven for 40 to 45 minutes, or until golden brown. Turn the buns out on a wire cake rack and serve warm or at room temperature.

Baking-Powder Biscuits

To make about 10

2 teaspoons butter, softened plus 8 tablespoons butter, cut into ¼-inch bits	2 teaspoons double-acting baking powder
2 cups all-purpose flour	1 teaspoon salt
	⅔ cup milk

Preheat the oven to 400°. With a pastry brush, spread the 2 teaspoons of softened butter evenly over a baking sheet. Set aside.

Combine the flour, baking powder and salt and sift them into a deep bowl. Add the 8 tablespoons of butter bits and rub the flour and fat together with your fingertips until they resemble flakes of coarse meal. Pour in the milk all at once and mix briefly with a wooden spoon, stirring just long enough to form a smooth soft dough that can be gathered into a compact ball. Do not overbeat.

Place the dough on a lightly floured surface and roll or pat it into a rough circle about ½-inch thick. With a biscuit cutter or the rim of a glass, cut the dough into 2½-inch rounds. Gather the scraps into a ball, pat or roll it out as before and cut as many more biscuits as you can.

Arrange the biscuits side by side on the buttered baking sheet and bake in the middle of the oven for about 20 minutes, or until they are a delicate golden brown. Serve at once.

ADDITIONAL INGREDIENTS FOR CHEESE-AND-HERB BISCUITS	Parmesan cheese
¼ freshly grated imported	¼ cup finely cut fresh chives
	¼ cup finely chopped fresh parsley

CHEESE-AND-HERB BISCUITS: Following precisely the directions for baking-powder biscuits, prepare the dough and gather it into a ball. While the dough is still in the bowl, knead into it the grated cheese, chives and parsley. Place the dough on a lightly floured surface, then roll, cut and bake the biscuits as described above.

Beaten Biscuits

By tradition, the dough for these biscuits is actually beaten with a mallet, hammer or even an ax for anywhere from 20 to 40 minutes. The recipe for this classic approach is described on page 50 of the main volume. However, putting the dough through a food grinder as described below is quicker and easier—and the biscuits themselves are enough like their beaten counterparts to please an old-time cook.

To make about 2 dozen
1½-inch biscuits

1 teaspoon butter, softened
2 cups flour
1½ teaspoons sugar

1 teaspoon salt
2 tablespoons lard, cut into ¼-inch bits
¼ cup milk combined with ¼ cup
   water

Preheat the oven to 400°. With a pastry brush, spread the softened butter evenly on a large baking sheet and set aside.

Combine the flour, sugar and salt, and sift them into a deep bowl. Drop in the lard and, with your fingers, rub the flour and fat together until they resemble flakes of coarse meal. Add the milk-and-water mixture, about 2 tablespoonfuls at a time, rubbing and kneading after each addition until the liquid is completely absorbed. Knead the dough vigorously in the bowl until it is smooth. Then put it through the coarsest blade of a food grinder four times, or until the dough is pliable and elastic.

To shape beaten biscuits the Maryland way, take a handful of the dough and squeeze your fingers into a fist, forcing the dough up between your thumb and forefinger. When it forms a ball about the size of a walnut, pinch it off and gently pat the dough into a flat round about ½ inch thick. To shape the biscuits as they do in Virginia, gather the dough into a ball and roll it out ½ inch thick on a lightly floured surface. With a biscuit cutter or the rim of a glass, cut the dough into 1½-inch rounds. Collect the scraps into a ball again, roll it out as before and cut as many more biscuits as you can.

Place the biscuits about 1 inch apart on the buttered baking sheet. Then prick the top of each one lightly with a three-tined fork to make a pattern of two or three parallel rows. Bake in the middle of the oven for about 20 minutes, or until the biscuits are a delicate golden color. Serve them at once with butter.

Fried Biscuits

In Maryland, these are called chicken biscuits and are fried in the fat remaining in the pan after the chicken is finished.

To make about a dozen 1½-inch
   biscuits

1 cup flour
2 teaspoons double-acting baking
   powder
¼ teaspoon salt
2 tablespoons butter, cut into bits
6 tablespoons milk
Lard or vegetable oil for frying

Combine the flour, baking powder and salt and sift them into a deep bowl. Add the butter bits and, with your fingers, rub the flour and fat together until they resemble flakes of coarse meal. Pour in the milk and toss lightly together with your fingers or a table fork.

Gather the dough into a ball and place it on a lightly floured surface. Then roll the dough about ¼ inch thick. With a biscuit cutter or the rim of a glass, cut the dough into 1½-inch rounds. Collect the scraps in a ball, roll them out again and cut as many more rounds as you can.

Melt 1½ pounds of lard in a heavy 12-inch skillet set over high heat. Or pour vegetable oil into a 12-inch skillet to a depth of about 1 inch. Heat the fat until it reaches a temperature of 375° on a deep-frying thermometer, or until it is very hot but not smoking. Fry the biscuits for about 4 or 5 minutes, turning them with a slotted spatula until they are evenly browned on both sides. Transfer them to paper towels to drain.

Serve at once. Traditionally, the biscuits are placed on the dinner plates with Maryland fried chicken and masked with gravy.

Virginia Ham Biscuits

To make about 16 two-inch biscuits

1 teaspoon vegetable shortening, softened, plus 4 tablespoons vegetable shortening, cut into ¼-inch bits
2 cups all-purpose flour
2 teaspoons double-acting baking powder
¼ teaspoon salt
½ cup finely ground Smithfield or country ham
¾ cup buttermilk

Preheat the oven to 425°. With a pastry brush spread the teaspoon of softened shortening evenly over a large baking sheet. Set aside.

Combine the flour, baking powder and salt, and sift them together into a deep bowl. Add the ham and shortening bits and, with your fingers, rub the flour and fat together until they resemble flakes of coarse meal. Pour in the buttermilk and toss together lightly until the dough can be gathered into a compact ball.

Place the ball on a lightly floured surface and pat or roll the dough into a rough circle about ½ inch thick. With a biscuit cutter or the rim of a glass, cut the dough into 2-inch rounds. Gather the scraps into a ball again, pat or roll them out as before, and cut out additional biscuits.

Place the biscuits about 1 inch apart on the greased baking sheet and bake in the middle of the oven for 20 to 25 minutes, or until they are golden brown. Transfer the biscuits to a heated platter and serve at once.

Hoecakes

To make eight 4-inch round cakes

1 cup white cornmeal, preferably water-ground
½ teaspoon salt
¾ cup boiling water
1 to 2 tablespoons bacon fat or butter

Combine the cornmeal and salt in a bowl. Stirring the mixture constantly with a spoon, pour in the boiling water in a slow, thin stream and beat until the batter is smooth. For each hoecake, scoop up 2 tablespoons of batter and pat it into a flat round about 4 inches in diameter.

In a heavy griddle or 10- to 12-inch skillet, melt 1 tablespoon of the bacon fat or butter over high heat. When the fat is very hot but not smoking, reduce the heat to low. Add 4 of the hoecakes and fry for about 2 minutes on each side until they are golden brown, turning them with a wide metal spatula. Transfer the crisp, browned cakes to a heated platter, add more fat to the pan if needed, and fry the remaining 4 cakes.

Serve the hoecakes at once, accompanied by sweet butter or cane syrup.

Hush Puppies

To make 18 to 20

¼ cup flour
4 teaspoons double-acting baking
   powder
½ teaspoon salt
1½ cups white cornmeal,
   preferably water-ground
2 eggs
¾ to 1 cup buttermilk
1 tablespoon finely chopped onions
1 teaspoon finely chopped garlic
Lard or vegetable oil for deep
   frying

Combine the flour, baking powder and salt and sift them together into a deep bowl. Stir in the cornmeal, unsifted, then add the eggs, one at a time, and beat vigorously with a wooden spoon until the mixture is smooth. Pour in ¾ cup of the buttermilk and stir until it is completely absorbed. If the batter seems dense, add up to ¼ cup more buttermilk by the spoonful until the batter holds its shape in a spoon. Beat in the finely chopped onions and garlic.

Preheat the oven to its lowest setting. Line a large shallow baking dish with a double thickness of paper towels and place the baking dish in the middle of the oven.

In a deep fryer or large heavy saucepan, melt enough lard to fill the pan to a depth of 2 to 3 inches, or pour in vegetable oil to a depth of 2 to 3 inches. Heat the fat until it reaches a temperature of 375° on a deep-frying thermometer.

To shape each hush puppy, scoop up a rounded tablespoon of the batter and push it into the hot fat with another spoon. Deep-fry the hush puppies 4 or 5 at a time, turning them about frequently with a slotted spoon for about 3 minutes, or until they are golden brown. Transfer them to the lined baking dish to drain and keep them warm in the low oven while you deep-fry the rest.

Serve the hush puppies hot, accompanied by butter. Traditionally hush puppies accompany fried fish.

DESSERTS & CANDIES

Syllabub

Syllabub was originally an English drink, closely related to egg nog. Its name is reputedly derived from wine that came from Sillery, in the Champagne region of France, and from "bub," which was Elizabethan English slang for a bubbly drink. Always made with wine, syllabub was considered by 18th- and 19th-Century American men to be a ladies' Christmas drink; they preferred the whiskey-based egg nog. In recent years syllabub has been served more frequently as a dessert, as described below. It may also be beaten very thick and used as a topping for fruits or cakes.

To serve 8

½ cup brandy
½ cup pale dry sherry
½ cup superfine sugar

¼ cup strained, fresh lemon juice
1 tablespoon finely grated fresh
   lemon peel
1 cup heavy cream

Combine the brandy, sherry, sugar, lemon juice and lemon peel in a large bowl. Mix well and set aside at room temperature for 15 to 20 minutes. Then stir in the cream and set aside for 15 minutes longer.

With a large wire whisk or a rotary beater, whip the mixture vigorously for about 1 minute until it begins to foam heavily on top. With a fine wire-mesh skimmer or slotted spoon, scoop the foam from the surface and place it gently in a wine or champagne glass. Beat the cream mixture for another minute or so, skim it as before and add the foam to the glass. Repeat until the glass is full; refrigerate it at once. Following this procedure, fill and immediately refrigerate 7 more glasses.

You may serve the syllabub at once or keep it in the refrigerator for as long as 12 hours. If you prefer to prepare this dessert well in advance, the glasses of syllabub can safely be kept in the freezer for 2 days.

Ginger Peach Ice Cream

To make about 1½ quarts

1½ teaspoons vanilla extract

4 cups heavy cream
¾ cup sugar
⅛ teaspoon salt

6 medium-sized firm ripe peaches
½ cup crystallized ginger, coarsely
   chopped

In a heavy 2- to 3-quart saucepan, heat 1 cup of the cream, the sugar and salt over low heat, stirring until the sugar is dissolved; do not let the mixture come to a boil. Pour the cream mixture into a deep bowl, stir in the remaining 3 cups of cream and the vanilla, and refrigerate until chilled.

Meanwhile, drop the peaches, 2 or 3 at a time, into enough boiling water to cover them completely and boil briskly for 2 to 3 minutes. With a slotted spoon, transfer the peaches to a sieve or colander and run cold water over them. Peel the peaches with a small sharp knife, halve them and discard the stones, then chop the fruit coarsely. Cover with foil or plastic wrap and refrigerate until ready to use.

Pack a 2-quart ice-cream freezer with layers of finely crushed or cracked ice and coarse rock salt in the proportions recommended by the freezer manufacturer. Add cold water if the manufacturer advises it. Then ladle the chilled cream mixture into the ice-cream can and cover it.

If you have a hand ice-cream maker, fill it with the chilled cream mixture and let it stand for 3 or 4 minutes before beginning to turn the handle. Then, beginning slowly at first, crank continuously for about 5 minutes. Stir in the peaches and ginger and crank for 10 to 15 minutes more. Do not stop turning at any time or the ice cream may be lumpy.

When the handle can barely be moved, the ice cream is ready to serve. If you wish to keep it for an hour or two, remove the lid and dasher. Scrape the ice cream off the dasher and pack it firmly into the container with a spoon. Cover securely, pour off any water in the bucket and repack the ice and salt solidly around it.

If you have an electric ice-cream maker, fill the can with the chilled cream mixture, cover it, turn on the switch and let the mixture churn for about 5 minutes. Stir in the peaches and ginger, cover again and continue to churn for about 10 to 15 minutes more, or until the motor slows or actually stops. Serve the ice cream immediately or follow the procedure above to keep it for an hour or two.

Lacking an ice-cream maker, stir the peaches and ginger into the chilled cream mixture and pour the mixture into two ice-cube trays from which the dividers have been removed. Spread the ice cream evenly and smooth the top with a rubber spatula. Freeze for 3 to 4 hours, stirring every 30 minutes or so and scraping into the ice cream the ice particles that form around the edges of the tray.

Tightly covered, the ice cream may safely be kept in the freezing compartment of the refrigerator for several weeks. Before serving, place it in the refrigerator for 20 to 30 minutes to let it soften slightly so that it can more easily be served.

Peppermint Stick Candy Ice Cream

To make 1½ quarts

6 ounces peppermint stick candy, 3 ounces pulverized in a blender or finely crushed with a rolling pin and 3 ounces finely chopped
½ cup sugar
1 quart heavy cream
1½ teaspoons vanilla extract

Combine the pulverized peppermint stick candy, the sugar and 1 cup of the cream in a heavy 1½- to 2-quart saucepan. Then set the pan over low heat and stir until the sugar dissolves completely. Remove the pan from the heat and stir in the vanilla extract and the remaining 3 cups of cream. Refrigerate the cream mixture until it is thoroughly chilled.

Pack a 2-quart ice-cream freezer with layers of finely crushed or cracked ice and coarse rock salt in the proportions recommended by the manufacturers, adding cold water if the directions call for it.

If you have a hand ice-cream maker, fill it with the ice-cream mixture, and let it stand for 3 or 4 minutes. Then turn the handle, starting slowly at first, and crank continuously for a few minutes. Add the chopped peppermint stick candy and continue to crank for 10 minutes longer. Do not stop turning or the ice cream may be lumpy. When the handle can barely be moved, the ice cream is ready to serve. If you wish to keep it for an hour or two, remove the lid and dasher. Scrape the ice cream off the dasher and pack it firmly in the container. Cover securely, pour off any water in the bucket and repack the ice and salt solidly around it.

If you have an electric ice-cream maker, fill the can with the ice-cream mixture, cover the can, turn it on and let it churn for about 5 minutes. Add the chopped candy, cover again and continue to churn for 10 minutes longer, or until the motor slows or actually stops. Serve the ice cream immediately or follow the procedure above to keep it for an hour or two.

Lacking an ice-cream maker, pour the ice-cream mixture and chopped candy into 2 ice-cube trays without their dividers, spreading it evenly. Freeze for about 6 hours, stirring every 30 minutes or so and scraping into it the ice particles that form around the edges of the tray.

Tightly covered, the ice cream may safely be kept in the freezer for several weeks. Before serving, place it in the refrigerator for 20 or 30 minutes to let it soften slightly so that it can be easily served.

Bishop Whipple's Pudding

To serve 8

1 tablespoon unsalted butter, softened
2 eggs
½ cup sugar
⅔ cup all-purpose flour
1 teaspoon baking powder
½ teaspoon vanilla extract

¼ pound (1 cup) pecans, coarsely chopped
6 ounces (1 cup) pitted dates, coarsely chopped
1 cup heavy cream, chilled
2 tablespoons dry sherry

Bishop Henry Benjamin Whipple, for whom this dessert is believed to have been named, was the late 19th Century bishop of what is now Minnesota. Also known as "the Bishop of All Outdoors," he traveled in the South for his health and kept a detailed diary of what he saw and ate.

Preheat the oven to 350°. Brush the bottom and sides of a 1-quart soufflé or baking dish with the tablespoon of softened butter and set aside.

In a large mixing bowl, beat the eggs with a wire whisk or a rotary or electric beater until they are frothy. Beat in the sugar, then the flour and baking powder. Add the vanilla, nuts and dates, and continue to beat until the ingredients are well combined. Pour the mixture into the prepared mold and bake in the center of the oven for about 25 minutes, or until the pudding no longer wobbles when the mold is shaken gently. Remove the pudding from the oven and cool for about 15 minutes.

In a large bowl, whip the heavy cream with a wire whisk or a rotary or electric beater until it is stiff enough to form soft peaks on the beater when lifted out of the bowl. Stir the sherry into the whipped cream and present in a small bowl along with the pudding.

Kentucky Fried Peaches

To serve 4

2 large firm ripe peaches
2 tablespoons unsalted butter

4 tablespoons sugar
2 tablespoons (1 ounce) bourbon

Drop the peaches into enough boiling water to cover them completely and boil briskly for 2 or 3 minutes. Then, with a slotted spoon, transfer the peaches to a sieve or colander to drain. Peel them with a small sharp knife, cut them in half, and remove the pits. Pat the halved peaches dry with paper towels.

In an 8- to 10-inch enameled or stainless-steel skillet, combine the butter and sugar over moderate heat. Stir constantly with a wooden spoon until the butter melts, then add the peaches, cut side down. Cook uncovered for 2 to 3 minutes, or until the bottoms of the peaches are golden. Turn them over with a spatula, baste with the sugar and butter in the pan, and cook for an additional 2 minutes.

Warm the bourbon in a ladle or small saucepan, then, stepping back, ignite it with a match and pour it into the pan of peaches. Gently slide the pan back and forth over the heat until the flames die. Serve at once, as an accompaniment to game or fowl, or as dessert.

Blackberry Cobbler
To serve 4 to 6

1 pint fresh blackberries, or substitute 2 cups frozen blackberries, thoroughly defrosted and drained	1 cup sugar
	2 eggs
	¾ cup milk
	1 teaspoon vanilla extract
1 cup all-purpose flour	1 teaspoon grated lemon rind
2 teaspoons double-acting baking powder	1½ cups heavy cream, chilled
	2 tablespoons confectioners' sugar

Preheat the oven to 350°. If you are using fresh blackberries, wash them in a colander set under cold running water, discarding any stems or blemished fruit. Spread the fresh or defrosted frozen berries on paper towels and pat them completely dry with additional towels. Then pour the berries into a 2-quart ovenproof mold or soufflé dish and set aside.

Sift the flour and baking powder into a large mixing bowl and drop in the sugar, eggs, milk, vanilla and lemon rind. With a wooden spoon, beat the ingredients briskly until they are thoroughly combined. Pour the batter over the berries and bake in the center of the oven for one hour, or until the top is crusty brown. Remove the cobbler from the oven and let it rest while you whip the cream.

With a whisk or a rotary or electric beater, beat the cream until it foams. Then beat in the confectioners' sugar and continue to beat until the cream forms soft peaks when the beater is lifted out of the bowl. Serve the cobbler hot, accompanied by a bowl of the whipped cream.

Lime Sherbet

To make about 1 pint

2 tablespoons plus 2 cups cold water
1 teaspoon unflavored gelatin
2 cups sugar

2 cups strained fresh lime juice
¼ teaspoon salt
2 drops green food coloring
2 egg whites

Pour the 2 tablespoons of cold water into a small bowl and sprinkle the gelatin over it to soften.

Combine the remaining 2 cups of water and the sugar in a small heavy saucepan and boil over high heat for about 5 minutes, stirring until the sugar dissolves and the syrup becomes completely clear. Thoroughly stir in the gelatin, remove the pan from the heat, and add the lime juice, salt and food coloring. Pour into a bowl and cool to room temperature. Then pour the mixture into 2 ice-cube trays from which the dividers have been removed. Freeze for 1 to 1½ hours, or until solid particles begin to form on the bottom and sides of the tray. Beat the sherbet briskly with the flat of a fork and return it to the freezer for 1 to 1½ hours more.

With a wire whisk or a rotary or electric beater, beat the egg whites until stiff enough to stand in unwavering peaks on the beater when lifted from the bowl. With a rubber spatula, scrape the sherbet into a deep bowl. Scoop the egg whites over the sherbet and fold them together thoroughly, return the lime sherbet to the ice-cube trays, smooth the tops with a spatula and freeze for 2 or 3 hours longer until the finished sherbet has a fine snowy texture.

To serve, spoon the sherbet into parfait glasses or dessert dishes.

Wine Jelly

To serve 4

2 envelopes unflavored gelatin
½ cup water
1 cup dry sherry

A pinch of salt
¼ cup strained fresh lemon juice
¼ cup strained fresh orange juice
⅔ cup sugar

In a small heatproof bowl, sprinkle the gelatin over the ½ cup of water. When the gelatin has softened for about 5 minutes, set the bowl in a skillet of simmering water and cook over low heat, stirring constantly, until the gelatin dissolves. Remove the skillet from the heat, but to keep the gelatin fluid, leave the bowl in the water.

In a large mixing bowl, combine the sherry, salt, lemon juice, orange juice and sugar, and stir with a wooden spoon until the sugar dissolves. Then stir in the warm gelatin and, when it is completely absorbed, pour the mixture into 4 individual dessert dishes. Refrigerate for at least 6 hours, or until the wine jelly is firm.

Divinity Candies

To make about 24

2 cups sugar	2 egg whites
½ cup water	½ teaspoon vanilla extract
⅓ cup light corn syrup	1½ cups coarsely chopped pecans

Combine the sugar, water and corn syrup in a heavy 1½- to 2-quart saucepan and bring to a boil over high heat, stirring until the sugar dissolves. Then cook briskly, uncovered and undisturbed, for 10 to 15 minutes, until the syrup reaches a temperature of 255° on a candy thermometer, or until a drop spooned into ice water immediately forms a compact and almost brittle ball.

Meanwhile, in a deep bowl, beat the egg whites with a wire whisk or a rotary or electric beater until they are stiff enough to stand in unwavering peaks on the beater when it is lifted from the bowl.

As soon as the syrup reaches the proper temperature, remove the pan from the heat. Whipping the egg whites constantly with the whisk or beater, pour in the syrup in a very slow, thin stream. (Do not scrape the saucepan; the syrup that clings to it is likely to be too sugary.) Add the vanilla and continue to beat for about 10 minutes longer, or until the candy begins to lose its gloss and is thick enough to hold its shape almost solidly in a spoon. Immediately stir in the pecans.

Without waiting a moment, drop the divinity by the tablespoon onto wax paper, letting each spoonful mound slightly in the center. Allow the candy to stand undisturbed until it is firm.

Ambrosia

To serve 6

4 large seedless oranges, peeled
2 cups freshly shredded coconut, or
   substitute 2 cups finely shredded
   packaged coconut
¼ cup sugar

With a small sharp knife, peel the oranges deeply enough to remove all of the white pith. Slice the oranges crosswise into ⅛-inch-thick rounds and place them in a large serving bowl. Add the shredded coconut and sugar and, with a large wooden spoon, toss together lightly but thoroughly. Cover the bowl with plastic wrap and refrigerate at least 2 hours before serving.

Bourbon Balls

To make about 60 one-inch candies

8 one-ounce squares semisweet
  chocolate, coarsely chopped
60 vanilla wafers, pulverized in a
  blender or wrapped in a towel
  and finely crushed with a rolling
pin (about 3 cups)
1 cup finely chopped pecans
1⅔ cups sugar
½ cup bourbon
¼ cup light corn syrup

In a small heavy skillet, melt the chocolate over low heat, stirring almost constantly to prevent the bottom from scorching. Remove the pan from the heat and let the chocolate cool to lukewarm.

Combine the pulverized vanilla wafers, pecans and ⅔ cup of sugar in a deep bowl. Pour in the chocolate, bourbon and corn syrup and stir vigorously with a wooden spoon until the ingredients are well combined.

To shape each bourbon ball, scoop up about a tablespoon of the mixture and pat it into a ball about 1 inch in diameter. Roll the balls in the remaining cup of sugar and, when they are lightly coated on all sides, place them in a wide-mouthed 1-quart jar equipped with a securely fitting lid. Cut two rounds from a double thickness of paper towels to fit inside the lid of the jar. Moisten the paper rounds with a little additional bourbon and press them tightly into the lid.

Seal the jar with the paper-lined lid and set the bourbon balls aside at room temperature for 3 or 4 days before serving. Tightly covered, the bourbon balls can safely be kept for 3 to 4 weeks.

Kentucky Colonels

To make about 20 candies

4 tablespoons unsalted butter,
  softened
2 cups confectioners' sugar
3 tablespoons bourbon
2 ounces pecans, finely chopped
  (⅓ cup)
8 ounces (½ pound) semisweet
  chocolate

Cream the butter and sugar together by beating them against the sides of a deep bowl with the back of a spoon until the mixture is light and fluffy. Beat in the bourbon, a tablespoon at a time, then stir in the chopped pecans. One at a time pinch off about 1 tablespoon of the mixture and roll it between the palms of your hands until it forms a ball about 1 inch in diameter. Place the balls on a cookie sheet lined with wax paper and refrigerate for 30 minutes.

Meanwhile, in a heavy 1- to 1½-quart saucepan, melt the chocolate over low heat, stirring frequently to prevent it from coming to a boil. Remove from the heat and let it rest for about 10 minutes, until the chocolate is cool but still fluid.

Remove the candies from the refrigerator and, one at a time, spear them with a small skewer or two-pronged kitchen fork. Dip it into the melted chocolate, coating it thoroughly, then place it on the sheet of wax paper. When all of the candies have been coated with chocolate, refrigerate them again for at least 2 hours before serving.

Peanut Brittle

To make about 1¾ pounds

2 teaspoons unsalted butter, softened, plus 2 tablespoons unsalted butter, cut into bits
1½ cups sugar
⅔ cup light corn syrup

⅔ cup cold water
2 cups lightly salted toasted Spanish peanuts, unpeeled
1 teaspoon strained fresh lemon juice

With a pastry brush, lightly coat a 15-inch-long cookie sheet or jelly-roll pan with the 2 teaspoons of softened butter.

Combine the sugar, corn syrup and water in a heavy 1½- to 2-quart enameled or stainless-steel saucepan. Stirring constantly, cook over moderate heat until the sugar dissolves. Raise the heat and bring the syrup to a boil. Continue to boil uncovered until the syrup reaches a temperature of 300° on a candy thermometer, meanwhile brushing down the crystals that form on the sides of the pan with a pastry brush lightly moistened with cold water.

Remove the pan from the heat and, with a wooden spoon, quickly stir in the nuts, butter bits and lemon juice. Pour the mixture at once onto the cookie sheet or jelly-roll pan and set aside at room temperature for about 30 minutes, until the candy hardens. Break the peanut brittle into irregularly shaped pieces and serve at once, or wrap in plastic bags and store in a covered container.

CAKES & PIES

Poundcake

To make one 9-by-5-by-3-inch loaf

2 teaspoons plus ½ pound unsalted
   butter, softened
2 tablespoons plus 2½ cups all-
   purpose flour
1¼ cups sugar
6 large eggs
1 tablespoon grated lemon rind
2 teaspoons vanilla extract

The ingredients in the original recipes for poundcake were used in the proportions that gave the cake its name: one pound each of butter, sugar, eggs and flour. The following recipe is more of a "half pound" cake, with the added fillip of lemon rind and vanilla.

Preheat the oven to 350°. With a pastry brush, spread 2 teaspoons of the softened butter evenly over the bottom and sides of a 9-by-5-by-3-inch loaf pan. Sprinkle the butter with 2 tablespoons of the flour and tip the pan from side to side to spread it evenly; then invert the pan and rap it sharply to remove the excess flour.

In a deep bowl, cream the remaining butter and the sugar together by mashing and beating them against the sides of the bowl with the back of a spoon until they are light and fluffy. Beat in the eggs, one at a time, then beat in the lemon rind and vanilla.

With a wooden spoon beat in the remaining flour, 1 cup at a time. When the flour is thoroughly incorporated and the batter is smooth, pour it into the prepared loaf pan, smoothing the top with a spatula. Bake in the center of the oven for 1 hour and 20 minutes, or until the cake begins to shrink away from the sides of the pan. Turn the cake out onto a wire rack and let it cool to room temperature.

Poundcake may be served in a variety of ways: alone, with whipped cream or ice cream, or as a breakfast cake with butter.

White Fruit Cake

To make one 6-pound cake

14 tablespoons butter, softened
3 cups flour
2 teaspoons double-acting baking
powder
½ teaspoon ground nutmeg,
preferably freshly grated
¾ teaspoon salt
2 cups golden raisins
¾ cup finely slivered candied
lemon peel (about 6 ounces)
¾ cup finely slivered candied
orange peel (about 6 ounces)
¾ cup finely slivered candied
pineapple (about 6 ounces)
¾ cup finely chopped candied
citron (about 6 ounces)
1 cup sugar
1¼ cups bourbon
1½ cups slivered blanched
almonds (about 6 ounces)
8 egg whites

Preheat the oven to 250°. With a pastry brush, spread 1 tablespoon of the softened butter over the bottom and sides of a 9-by-3-inch spring-form tube cake pan. Coat two strips of wax paper with another tablespoon of the butter and fit the strips around the tube and the sides of the pan, with the greased surfaces toward the center. Set aside.

Combine the flour, baking powder, nutmeg and salt and sift them together into a deep bowl. Add the raisins, lemon peel, orange peel, pineapple and citron, and toss the fruit about with a spoon until the pieces are evenly coated.

In another deep bowl, cream the remaining 12 tablespoons of butter and the sugar together, beating and mashing them against the sides of the bowl with the back of a large wooden spoon until the mixture is light and fluffy. Stir in the flour-and-fruit mixture a cup or so at a time. Then add ¾ cup of the bourbon and, when it is completely incorporated, stir in the slivered almonds.

With a wire whisk or a rotary or electric beater, beat the egg whites until they are stiff enough to stand in unwavering peaks on the beater when it is lifted from the bowl. Scoop the egg whites over the batter and, with a rubber spatula, fold them together gently but thoroughly.

Pour the batter into the paper-lined pan, filling it about three quarters full, and smooth the top with the spatula. Bake in the middle of the oven for 2½ to 3 hours, or until a toothpick or cake tester inserted in the center of the cake comes out clean.

Let the cake cool overnight before removing the sides of the spring-form. Then slip it off the bottom of the pan and carefully peel away the paper. Place the cake on a serving plate and sprinkle it evenly with the remaining ½ cup of bourbon. Wrap in cheesecloth and set the cake aside at room temperature for at least 24 hours before serving. Securely wrapped in foil or plastic, it can be kept for several months, and its flavor will improve with age.

Lane Cake

To make one 3-layer cake

CAKE

1 tablespoon plus ½ pound unsalted butter, softened	A pinch of salt
3 tablespoons plus 2½ cups all-purpose flour	¾ cup milk
	1 teaspoon vanilla extract
2 teaspoons double-acting baking powder	1½ cups sugar
	8 egg whites

CAKE: Preheat the oven to 350°. With a pastry brush, spread 1 tablespoon of the softened butter evenly over the bottom and sides of three 9-inch cake pans. Add 1 tablespoon of the flour to each pan and tip the pans from side to side to spread the flour evenly; then invert the pans and rap them sharply to remove the excess flour.

Combine the remaining 2½ cups of flour, the baking powder and salt, and sift them into a bowl. Stir the milk and vanilla extract together and set aside.

In a deep bowl, cream the remaining butter and the sugar together by beating and mashing them against the sides of the bowl with the back of a spoon until the mixture is light and fluffy. Beat in about 1 cup of the flour mixture and, when it is well incorporated, ¼ cup of the vanilla-flavored milk. Repeat twice more, alternating 1 cup of the flour mixture and ¼ cup of the milk each time. Continue to beat until the batter is completely smooth.

With a wire whisk or a rotary or electric beater, beat the 8 egg whites in a large bowl until they are firm enough to stand in soft peaks on the beater when it is lifted from the bowl. Stir a few tablespoons of the egg whites into the batter, then scoop the remaining batter over the whites and fold them together gently but thoroughly with a rubber spatula.

Pour the batter into the prepared pans, dividing it equally among them and smoothing the tops with the spatula. Bake in the middle of the oven for about 25 minutes, or until the cakes begin to shrink away from the sides of the pans and the tops spring back immediately when prodded gently with a finger. Turn the cakes out onto wire racks and let them cool to room temperature.

FILLING
8 egg yolks
1 cup sugar
A pinch of salt
1 cup brandy
8 tablespoons (1 quarter-pound
stick) butter, melted and cooled

1 cup seedless raisins, finely
chopped
¾ cup freshly grated coconut, or
substitute ¾ cup shredded
packaged coconut
1 cup finely chopped pecans
1 teaspoon vanilla extract

FILLING: In a deep bowl, beat the egg yolks, sugar and salt with a wire whisk or a rotary or electric beater for 3 or 4 minutes, or until the yolks form a slowly dissolving ribbon when the beater is lifted from the bowl. Whisking constantly, pour in the brandy in a slow, thin stream, then whisk in the melted butter. When thoroughly blended, transfer the mixture to a 1- to 1½-quart enameled or stainless-steel saucepan. Cook over low heat, stirring constantly, until the filling has thickened enough to coat a spoon lightly. Do not let the mixture come near a boil or it will curdle. Stir in the raisins, coconut, pecans and vanilla, and set the filling aside to cool to room temperature. Then cover with plastic wrap and refrigerate until ready to use.

BOILED ICING
2 egg whites
A pinch of salt
2 cups sugar

2 tablespoons light corn syrup
⅔ cup cold water

BOILED ICING: In a large mixing bowl, beat the egg whites and salt with a wire whisk or a rotary or electric beater until the whites are firm enough to stand in soft peaks when the beater is lifted from the bowl.

Combine the sugar, corn syrup and cold water in a heavy 1- to 1½-quart saucepan and, stirring frequently, cook over moderate heat until the sugar dissolves. Raise the heat to high and boil uncovered and undisturbed until the syrup reaches 240° on a candy thermometer. Remove the saucepan from the heat.

Beating constantly, pour the hot syrup over the beaten egg whites in a slow, thin stream, and continue to beat until the boiled icing is smooth, thick and cool.

TO ASSEMBLE: Set one cake layer on an inverted cake pan and, with a metal spatula or knife, spread about ¾ cup of the filling over it. Carefully set the second cake layer in place and spread with the remaining filling. Top with the third cake layer, and coat the top and sides with the boiled icing. Slide the cake onto a serving plate and serve. Or, if you prefer, cover loosely with wax paper or aluminum foil and set aside at room temperature for as long as two days; the filling will keep the cake moist.

Coconut Cake with Lemon Filling

To make one 9-inch 4-layer cake

CAKE

2 tablespoons butter, softened	8 egg yolks
2 tablespoons plus 2 cups flour, sifted before measuring	2 cups sugar
	¼ cup strained fresh lemon juice
1 teaspoon double-acting baking powder	2 teaspoons finely grated fresh lemon peel
⅛ teaspoon salt	8 egg whites

Preheat the oven to 350°. With a pastry brush, spread the 2 tablespoons of softened butter over the bottom and sides of two 9-inch layer-cake pans. Add 1 tablespoon of flour to each pan and, one at a time, tip the pans from side to side to distribute the flour evenly. Then invert each pan and rap it sharply to remove the excess flour.

Combine the 2 cups of sifted flour, the teaspoon of baking powder and ⅛ teaspoon of salt and sift them together on a plate or on a sheet of wax paper. Set aside.

In a deep bowl, beat the egg yolks and 2 cups of sugar with a wire whisk or a rotary or electric beater for 4 to 5 minutes, or until the mixture is thick enough to fall back on itself in a slowly dissolving ribbon when the beater is lifted from the bowl. Beat in the ¼ cup lemon juice and 2 teaspoons lemon peel. Then add the flour mixture, about ½ cup at a time, beating well after each addition.

With a whisk or a rotary or electric beater, beat the 8 egg whites in another bowl until they are stiff enough to stand in unwavering peaks on the beater when it is lifted up out of the bowl. Scoop the egg whites over the batter and, with a rubber spatula, fold them gently but thoroughly together until no trace of white shows.

Pour the batter into the buttered and floured pans, dividing it equally between them and smoothing the tops with the spatula. Bake in the middle of the oven for about 20 minutes, or until a toothpick or cake tester inserted in the center of the cake comes out clean and dry. Let the cakes cool in the pans for about 5 minutes, then turn them out on wire racks to cool to room temperature.

FILLING

1½ cups sugar	¼-inch bits
¼ cup cornstarch	2 tablespoons finely grated fresh lemon peel
⅛ teaspoon salt	
2 eggs, lightly beaten	⅔ cup strained fresh lemon juice
2 tablespoons butter, cut into	1 cup water

Meanwhile, prepare the filling in the following fashion: Combine the

1½ cups sugar, the cornstarch, ⅛ teaspoon salt and the 2 beaten eggs in a heavy 1½- to 2-quart saucepan and mix well with a wire whisk or wooden spoon. Stir in the butter bits, 2 tablespoons lemon peel, ⅔ cup lemon juice and 1 cup water and, when all the ingredients are well blended, set the pan over high heat.

Stirring the filling mixture constantly, bring to a boil over high heat. Immediately reduce the heat to low and continue to stir until the filling is smooth and thick enough to coat the spoon heavily. Scrape the filling into a bowl with a rubber spatula, and let it cool to room temperature.

ICING

4 egg whites
½ cup confectioners' sugar
1 teaspoon vanilla extract

1½ cups white corn syrup
2 cups freshly grated, peeled coconut meat

When the cake and filling are cool, prepare the icing: With a wire whisk or a rotary or electric beater, beat the 4 egg whites until they are stiff enough to stand in soft peaks on the uplifted beater. Sprinkle them with the confectioners' sugar and vanilla and continue to beat until the egg whites are stiff and glossy.

In a small saucepan, bring the corn syrup to a boil over high heat and cook briskly until it reaches a temperature of 239° on a candy thermometer, or until a drop spooned into ice water immediately forms a soft ball. Beating the egg white mixture constantly with a wooden spoon, pour in the corn syrup in a slow, thin stream and continue to beat until the icing is smooth, thick and cool.

To assemble, cut each cake in half horizontally, thus creating four thin layers. Place one layer, cut side up, on an inverted cake or pie tin and, with a small metal spatula, spread about ⅓ of the lemon filling over it. Put another cake layer on top, spread with filling, and cover it with the third layer. Spread this layer with the remaining filling, and place the fourth layer on top.

Smooth the icing over the top and sides of the cake with the spatula. Then sprinkle the coconut generously on the top and, with your fingers, pat it into the sides of the cake. Carefully transfer the coconut cake to a serving plate and serve at once. If the cake must wait, drape waxed paper around the top and sides to keep the icing moist.

In Key West and other parts of the Deep South coconut cake is traditionally served at Christmastime.

Lady Baltimore Cake

Lady Baltimore cake is not, as one might imagine, from Baltimore, Mary-land, but was popularized at a leading Charleston, South Carolina, res-taurant, later named in honor of the cake.

To make one 3-layer cake

CAKE

2 tablespoons plus ½ pound unsalted butter, softened	¼ teaspoon salt
	1 cup milk
2 tablespoons plus 3 cups cake flour	1 teaspoon almond extract
1 tablespoon double-acting baking powder	1½ cups sugar
	5 egg whites

NOTE: Before making the cake, see the frosting section opposite for in-structions regarding the soaking of dried fruits and nuts.

CAKE: Preheat the oven to 350°. With a pastry brush, spread 2 table-spoons of the softened butter on the bottom and sides of three 9-inch layer-cake pans. Divide 2 tablespoons of the flour among the three pans and tip the pans from side to side to distribute the flour evenly. Then invert each pan and rap it sharply to remove the excess flour.

Combine the remaining flour, baking powder and salt, and sift them to-gether into a bowl. Stir the milk and almond extract together in a small bowl and set aside.

In a large deep bowl, cream the remaining butter and the sugar to-gether by beating them against the sides of the bowl with the back of a wooden spoon until the mixture is light and fluffy. Beat in about 1 cup of the flour mixture and, when it is well incorporated, beat in ⅓ cup of the milk-and-almond-extract mixture. Repeat twice more, alter-nating the flour and milk mixtures, and continue to beat until the bat-ter is smooth.

With a wire whisk or a rotary or electric beater, beat the 5 egg whites in a large bowl until they are firm enough to stand in stiff peaks on the beater when it is lifted out of the bowl. Stir a few tablespoons of the whites into the batter, then scoop the batter over the whites and fold to-gether gently but thoroughly with a rubber spatula.

Pour the batter into the pans, dividing it equally among them and smoothing the tops with the spatula. Bake in the middle of the oven for 25 to 30 minutes, until the tops of the cakes are pale gold and they have begun to shrink away from the sides of the pans. Turn the cake layers out onto the wire racks to cool to room temperature.

FROSTING

2 cups seedless raisins, finely chopped	4 egg whites
2 cups walnuts, finely chopped	¼ teaspoon cream of tartar
12 figs, pitted and finely chopped	3 cups sugar
1 cup sherry	1 cup water
	1 tablespoon light corn syrup

FROSTING: At least 3 hours before you plan to make the filling, place the raisins, walnuts and figs in a bowl. Pour in the sherry and soak the mixture at room temperature, tossing frequently with a wooden spoon.

With a wire whisk or a rotary or electric beater, beat the 4 egg whites and cream of tartar in a deep bowl until they are firm enough to stand in stiff peaks on the beater when it is lifted from the bowl.

Quickly combine the sugar, water and corn syrup in a heavy 1- to 1½-quart enameled or stainless-steel saucepan and, stirring frequently, cook over moderate heat until the sugar dissolves. Raise the heat and continue to cook uncovered and undisturbed until the syrup reaches 238° on a candy thermometer, or until a few drops spooned into ice water immediately form a soft ball.

Beating the reserved egg whites constantly, pour in the hot syrup in a slow, thin stream, and continue to beat until the filling is smooth, thick and cool.

Place the raisins, nuts and figs in a fine sieve and drain them. Discard the soaking liquid. Stir the fruit and nuts into the frosting.

TO ASSEMBLE: Set one cake layer upside down on an inverted cake pan and, with a metal spatula or knife, spread about ½ cup of the frosting evenly over the surface of the cake. Carefully put the second cake layer in place right side up, and spread with another ½ cup of the frosting. Top with the third cake layer right side up and coat the top and sides of the cake with the remaining frosting. Carefully slide the cake onto a serving plate and serve. Or, if you prefer, cover loosely with wax paper or aluminum foil and set aside at room temperature for as long as 2 days; frosting will keep the cake moist.

Robert E. Lee Cake

This cake was much esteemed by the great Confederate general whose name it bears.

To make one 9-inch 4-layer cake

CAKE

2 tablespoons butter, softened

2 tablespoons unsifted flour, plus 2 cups flour, sifted before measuring

1 teaspoon double-acting baking powder

⅛ teaspoon salt

8 egg yolks

2 cups sugar

¼ cup strained fresh lemon juice

2 teaspoons finely grated fresh lemon peel

8 egg whites

Preheat the oven to 350°. With a pastry brush, spread the 2 tablespoons of softened butter over the bottom and sides of two 9-inch layer-cake pans. Add a tablespoon of the unsifted flour to each pan and one at a time tip the pans from side to side to distribute the flour evenly. Then invert the pans and rap them sharply to remove the excess flour.

Combine the 2 cups sifted flour, the baking powder and salt, and sift them together onto a plate or sheet of wax paper. Set aside.

In a deep bowl, beat the 8 egg yolks and 2 cups of sugar with a wire whisk or a rotary or electric beater for 4 to 5 minutes, or until the mixture is thick enough to fall back on itself in a slowly dissolving ribbon when the beater is lifted from the bowl. Beat in the ¼ cup lemon juice and 2 teaspoons lemon peel. Then add the flour mixture about ½ cup at a time, beating well after each addition.

With a whisk or a rotary or electric beater, beat the egg whites in another bowl until they are stiff enough to stand in unwavering peaks on the beater when it is lifted out of the bowl. Scoop the egg whites over the batter and, with a rubber spatula, fold them together gently but thoroughly.

Pour the batter into the pans, dividing it equally between them and smoothing the tops with the spatula. Bake in the middle of the oven for about 20 minutes, or until a toothpick or cake tester inserted in the center of the cake comes out clean. Let the cakes cool in the pans for about 5 minutes, then turn them out on wire racks to cool to room temperature.

FILLING

6 tablespoons unsalted butter, cut into ¼-inch bits
¾ cup sugar
¾ cup strained fresh lemon juice
6 egg yolks
4 teaspoons finely grated fresh lemon peel

Meanwhile, prepare the filling in the following fashion: Combine the butter bits, ¾ cup sugar, ¾ cup lemon juice, and 6 egg yolks in a heavy 1½- to 2-quart saucepan. Stirring constantly, cook over the lowest possible heat until the mixture thickens enough to coat the back of a spoon heavily. Do not let the mixture boil or the yolks will curdle. With a rubber spatula, scrape the filling into a small bowl and stir in the 4 teaspoons of lemon peel. Let the filling cool to room temperature.

FROSTING

4 tablespoons butter, softened
3½ cups (1 pound) confectioners' sugar
¼ cup strained fresh orange juice combined with 2 tablespoons strained fresh lemon juice
1 egg yolk
¼ cup finely grated fresh orange peel
2 teaspoons finely grated fresh lemon peel

When the cake and filling are cool, prepare the frosting: In a large bowl, cream the 4 tablespoons of softened butter by beating and mashing it against the sides of the bowl with a wooden spoon until it is light and fluffy. Beat in about 1 cup of the confectioners' sugar and, when it is completely incorporated, add 2 tablespoons of the fresh juice mixture. Repeat two more times, alternating 1¼ cups of the sugar with 2 tablespoons of the juice and beating well after each addition. Mix in the egg yolk, the ¼ cup of orange peel and the 2 teaspoons lemon peel.

To assemble, cut each cake in half horizontally, thus creating four thin layers. Place one layer, cut side up, on an inverted cake or pie tin and, with a small metal spatula, spread about one third of the lemon filling over it. Put another layer on top, spread with filling, and cover it with the third layer. Spread with the remaining filling, and place the fourth cake layer on top.

Smooth the remaining frosting over the top and sides of the cake with the spatula. Then carefully transfer the Robert E. Lee cake to a large circular cake plate.

Kossuth Cake

MELON-MOLD CAKE WITH CHOCOLATE SAUCE

Kossuth cake, originally made as individual cream-filled spongecakes, was reportedly created by a Baltimore confectioner in honor of a visit in 1851 by Louis Kossuth, the Hungarian patriot who had led his country in a revolt against Austrian rule. The cake enjoyed far more success than Kossuth's attempt to raise money for a new revolt.

To serve 6 to 8

CAKE

7 tablespoons unsalted butter,
    softened
2 tablespoons all-purpose flour
3 cups cake flour, not the self-rising
    type
1 tablespoon double-acting baking
    powder
⅛ teaspoon salt
1 cup milk
1 tablespoon vanilla extract
2 cups sugar
3 eggs

CAKE: Preheat the oven to 350°. With a pastry brush, spread 1 tablespoon of the softened butter evenly over the bottom and sides of a 2-quart melon mold and the inside of its lid. Sprinkle the 2 tablespoons of all-purpose flour over the mold and the inside of its lid and tip them from side to side to spread the flour evenly; then invert the mold and lid and rap them sharply to remove the excess flour.

Combine the cake flour, baking powder and salt, and sift them into a bowl. Stir together the milk and vanilla and set aside.

In a deep bowl, cream the remaining butter and the sugar together by beating and mashing them against the sides of the bowl with the back of a large spoon until the mixture is light and fluffy. Beat in the eggs, one at a time, and continue to beat until they are thoroughly absorbed. Beat in 1 cup of the flour mixture and, when it is well incorporated, ⅓ cup of the vanilla-flavored milk. Repeat twice more, alternating the flour and milk in similar amounts. When all the ingredients have been added, continue to beat until the batter is smooth. Pour the batter into the melon mold and cover the mold securely with its lid. Carefully fit the rounded bottom of the mold into one of the slots of an oven rack to steady it, and bake in the center of the oven for 1½ hours.

Remove the mold from the oven, lift off the lid, and turn the cake out onto a cake rack to cool to room temperature. Then, with a serrated knife, cut off the flat base of the cake about 1½ inches from the bottom. With a large spoon, scoop out the soft insides of both the cake and the base, leaving only a 1-inch-thick shell in both.

FILLING
1 cup heavy cream, chilled
¼ cup confectioners' sugar

FILLING: With a wire whisk or a rotary or electric beater, beat the heavy cream in a large chilled bowl until it begins to thicken. Sprinkle with the confectioners' sugar and continue to beat until the cream is firm enough to stand in stiff peaks on the beater when it is lifted out of the bowl. Spoon the whipped cream into the cake shell, replace the flat base, and carefully invert the cake so that it sits firmly on the base. Wrap in wax paper and refrigerate for at least 1 hour, or until ready to serve.

CHOCOLATE SAUCE
1 cup sugar
¼ cup heavy cream
¼ cup milk
4 ounces (4 squares) semisweet
    chocolate, finely chopped
1 tablespoon unsalted butter, cut
    into bits
1 tablespoon vanilla extract
Confectioners' sugar

CHOCOLATE SAUCE: In a 1½- to 2-quart enameled or stainless-steel saucepan, combine the sugar, cream and milk over moderate heat, stirring constantly until the sugar dissolves. Stir in the chocolate, then stir in the butter bits and vanilla. Continue to cook over moderate heat for another minute or two, stirring frequently, until the chocolate melts and the sauce thickens lightly. Remove from the heat and cool to lukewarm.

To serve, sprinkle the cake liberally with confectioners' sugar and serve with a bowl or sauceboat of the warm chocolate sauce.

Huckleberry Cake

To make one 8-inch cake

2 teaspoons butter, softened, plus
    8 tablespoons (1 quarter-pound
    stick) unsalted butter, softened
1 tablespoon plus 2 cups all-purpose
    flour
1 cup sugar
3 egg yolks
1 teaspoon grated lemon rind

1 teaspoon baking powder
½ teaspoon ground nutmeg
½ teaspoon ground cinnamon
½ cup milk
1 pint fresh huckleberries, or
    substitute blueberries, washed,
    thoroughly drained, and patted
    dry with paper towels
3 egg whites

Preheat the oven to 350°. With a pastry brush, spread the 2 teaspoons of butter evenly over the bottom and sides of an 8-inch springform pan at least 2 inches deep. Sprinkle a tablespoon of flour into the pan, tipping it from side to side to coat the bottom and sides evenly. Then invert the pan and rap it sharply on the table to remove any excess flour.

In a deep bowl, cream the remaining butter and the sugar together, beating and mashing them against the sides of the bowl with the back of a wooden spoon until the mixture is light and fluffy. Beat in the egg yolks, one at a time, then beat in the lemon rind.

Sift the remaining flour, baking powder, nutmeg and cinnamon together into a large bowl. Remove 3 tablespoons of the mixture and set aside. Beat about ⅓ cup of the remaining flour mixture into the creamed butter and sugar and, when it is well incorporated, beat in 2 tablespoons of the milk. Repeat three more times, adding about ⅓ cup of the flour mixture alternately with 2 tablespoons of the milk, and continue to beat until all the flour and milk are incorporated and the batter is smooth.

Sprinkle the dried berries with the reserved 3 tablespoons of the flour mixture and gently toss with a rubber spatula until they are lightly coated. With the spatula, fold the berries into the batter.

With a wire whisk or a rotary or electric beater, beat the egg whites until they are firm enough to stand in soft peaks on the beater when it is lifted from the bowl. Stir a few tablespoons of the egg whites into the batter, then scoop the remaining batter over the whites and fold them together gently but thoroughly with the spatula.

Pour the batter into the springform pan and smooth the top with the spatula. Bake the cake in the middle of the oven for about 1 hour and 20 minutes, or until the top is golden brown and the cake has begun to shrink away from the sides of the pan. Remove the sides of the pan and let the cake cool before serving.

Huguenot Torte

To serve 8 to 10

1 tablespoon butter, softened
¼ cup flour
1 teaspoon double-acting baking
  powder
¼ teaspoon salt
3 eggs
1½ cups sugar
1 teaspoon vanilla extract
1 cup finely chopped peeled apples
1 cup plus 2 tablespoons finely
  chopped pecans
1 cup heavy cream, chilled

Preheat the oven to 400°. With a pastry brush, spread the softened butter evenly over the bottom and sides of a baking-serving dish 12 inches long, 8 inches wide and 2 to 3 inches deep. Combine the flour, baking powder and salt and sift them together onto a plate or a sheet of wax paper. Set aside.

With a wire whisk or a rotary or electric beater, beat the eggs, sugar and vanilla for 4 to 5 minutes until the mixture is thick enough to fall in a slowly dissolving ribbon when the beater is lifted from the bowl. Beat in the flour mixture. Then add the chopped apples and 1 cup of the chopped pecans and fold them into the batter gently but thoroughly with a rubber spatula.

Pour the batter into the buttered baking dish and smooth the top with the spatula. Bake in the middle of the oven for 30 to 35 minutes, or until a toothpick or cake tester inserted in the center comes out clean. Remove the torte from the oven and let it cool slightly.

Meanwhile, in a chilled bowl, beat the cream with a wire whisk or a rotary or electric beater until it is stiff enough to stand in unwavering peaks on the beater when lifted out of the bowl. Spoon the whipped cream into a serving bowl and sprinkle the top with the remaining 2 tablespoons of the chopped pecans.

Serve the Huguenot torte while it is still warm, directly from the baking dish, scooping out the portions crust side up with a serving spoon or spatula. Present the whipped cream separately.

Tennessee Jam Cake

To make a 9-inch 3-layer cake

CAKE

3 tablespoons plus ½ pound
    butter, softened
3 cups all-purpose flour
1 tablespoon baking soda
1 tablespoon ground cinnamon
1 tablespoon ground allspice

1½ cups seedless blackberry jam
1 cup strawberry preserves
1 cup sugar
5 egg yolks, lightly beaten
1 cup buttermilk
5 egg whites

Preheat the oven to 350°. With a pastry brush, spread the 3 tablespoons of softened butter evenly over the bottoms and sides of three 9-inch layer-cake pans. Set aside.

Combine the flour, soda, cinnamon and allspice, and sift them together onto a plate or a sheet of wax paper. Combine the blackberry jam and strawberry preserves and, with a wooden spoon, rub them through a fine sieve into a small bowl. Set aside.

In a deep bowl, cream the remaining ½ pound of softened butter and the sugar together, beating and mashing them against the sides of the bowl with the back of a spoon until the mixture is light and fluffy. Beat in the egg yolks and then add the sieved jam mixture.

Add about 1 cup of the flour mixture and, when it is well incorporated, stir in ⅓ cup of the buttermilk. Repeat two more times, alternating 1 cup of flour with ⅓ cup of buttermilk, and continue to beat until the batter is smooth.

With a wire whisk or a rotary or electric beater, beat the 5 egg whites until they are stiff enough to form unwavering peaks on the beater when it is lifted from the bowl. Scoop the egg whites over the batter and, with a rubber spatula, fold them together gently but thoroughly.

Pour the batter into the buttered cake pans, dividing it evenly among them and smoothing the tops with the rubber spatula. Bake in the middle of the oven for 40 minutes, or until a toothpick or cake tester inserted in the center of the cake comes out clean. Let the cakes cool for about 5 minutes, then turn them out onto wire racks to cool to room temperature.

ICING

4 egg whites
A pinch of salt
6 cups confectioners' sugar, sifted

1 teaspoon vanilla extract
¼ teaspoon almond extract
½ cup coarsely chopped pecans

To prepare the icing, beat the 4 egg whites and salt together in a deep bowl with a wire whisk or a rotary or electric beater until they are stiff enough to form soft peaks on the uplifted beater. Add the confectioners' sugar, about ½ cup at a time, beating well after each addition and continue to beat until the icing is smooth and fluffy. Beat in the vanilla and almond extract, then stir in the pecans.

To assemble, place one layer of the cooled cake on a serving plate. With a small metal spatula, spread about ½ inch of icing evenly over the layer. Put another layer on top, ice and cover it with the third layer. Then spread the remaining icing over the top and sides of the cake. Cover the cake loosely with wax paper and set aside at room temperature for 1 to 3 days before serving.

Buttermilk Coffeecake

BISHOP'S BREAD

To make one 9-inch cake

1 teaspoon unsalted butter, softened, plus 12 tablespoons unsalted butter, cut into bits
1 tablespoon plus 2 cups sifted all-purpose flour
1½ teaspoons baking powder
1 cup light brown sugar
⅔ cup buttermilk
1 egg, lightly beaten
½ cup finely chopped pecans or almonds
1 teaspoon ground cinnamon
½ cup currants

Preheat the oven to 425°. With a pastry brush, brush the bottom and sides of a 9-inch layer-cake pan with the teaspoon of softened butter. Add 1 tablespoon of flour and tip the pan to distribute it evenly. Then invert the pan and rap it sharply to dislodge the excess flour.

In a large mixing bowl, combine the rest of the flour, the baking powder, brown sugar and butter bits, and rub them together with your fingertips until they look like fine crumbs. Set aside ½ cup of the mixture to be used for the topping.

Into the mixture remaining in the bowl gradually stir the buttermilk, egg, nuts, cinnamon and currants. When the ingredients are well combined and the batter is smooth, pour it into the pan and sprinkle the top evenly with the reserved crumb mixture. Bake the cake in the center of the oven for 15 minutes, then reduce the heat to 375°. Bake for an additional 20 to 25 minutes, or until a small knife inserted in the center comes out clean. Serve the coffeecake warm or at room temperature.

Fried Peach Turnovers

To make about 2 dozen

2 cups flour
1 teaspoon baking powder
½ teaspoon salt
8 tablespoons butter, chilled and cut
   into ¼-inch bits
6 to 8 tablespoons ice water
8 medium-sized firm ripe peaches
   (about 2 pounds)

½ cup granulated sugar
¼ cup water
½ teaspoon ground cinnamon
¼ teaspoon ground nutmeg
Lard or vegetable oil for deep
   frying
½ cup confectioners' sugar

Combine the flour, baking powder and salt and sift them into a deep bowl. Add the butter bits and, with your fingertips, rub the flour and fat together until they resemble flakes of coarse meal. Pour in 6 tablespoons of the ice water all at once, toss lightly and gather the dough into a ball. If the dough seems crumbly, add up to 2 tablespoons more ice water a few drops at a time until all the particles adhere. Dust the dough with flour, wrap it in wax paper and refrigerate at least 1 hour before using.

Meanwhile, drop the peaches, 3 or 4 at a time, into enough boiling water to cover them completely. Boil briskly for 2 to 3 minutes, then with a slotted spoon, transfer the peaches to a sieve or colander to drain, and peel them with a small sharp knife. Cut the peaches in half, discard the pits, and chop the fruit coarsely.

Combine the chopped peaches, granulated sugar and ¼ cup water in a 3- to 4-quart enameled or stainless-steel saucepan and bring to a boil over high heat, stirring with a wooden spoon until the sugar dissolves completely. Reduce the heat to moderate and, stirring from time to time, cook until the mixture is thick enough to hold its shape almost solidly in the spoon. With a rubber spatula, scrape the entire contents of the pan into a bowl, stir in the cinnamon and nutmeg and set the peaches aside to cool to room temperature.

On a lightly floured surface, roll the dough into a rough circle about 1/16 inch thick. With a cookie cutter or the rim of a glass, cut the dough into 4½-inch rounds. Gather the scraps into a ball, roll them out as before, and cut as many more rounds as you can.

To shape each turnover, place about 2 tablespoons of the peach mixture on the lower third of a round of dough. Moisten the edges of the round with a finger dipped in cold water, fold the round in half and press the edges tightly together to enclose the peach filling securely.

Preheat the oven to its lowest setting. Line a large shallow baking dish with a double thickness of paper towels and place it in the heated oven.

In a deep fryer or large heavy saucepan, melt enough lard to fill the pan to a depth of 2 or 3 inches, or pour in vegetable oil to a depth of 2 or 3 inches. Then heat the fat until it reaches a temperature of 375° on a deep-frying thermometer.

Deep-fry the turnovers, 3 or 4 at a time, turning them about occasionally with a slotted spoon for about 3 minutes, or until they are crisp and golden. As they brown, transfer the turnovers to the lined dish to drain and keep them warm in the oven while you deep-fry the rest.

Sprinkle the turnovers lightly with confectioners' sugar, arrange them on a heated platter and serve at once.

Chocolate Brownies with Peanuts

To make about 2 dozen

	3 eggs
2½ ounces (2½ squares) unsweetened chocolate	⅓ cup all-purpose flour
	½ teaspoon baking powder
12 tablespoons (1½ quarter-pound sticks) plus 1 tablespoon unsalted butter, softened	½ teaspoon salt
	1 teaspoon vanilla extract
	1 cup lightly salted Spanish peanuts,
1 cup sugar	unpeeled

Preheat the oven to 350°. Melt the chocolate in a small heavy saucepan over low heat, stirring constantly to prevent it from burning. Set aside to cool to room temperature.

Meanwhile, in a large mixing bowl cream the 12 tablespoons of butter and the sugar together by beating them against the sides of the bowl with a large spoon until the mixture is light and fluffy. Beat in the eggs, one at a time, and when they are completely absorbed, beat in the chocolate.

Sift the flour, baking powder and salt together into the mixture, and beat vigorously until the ingredients are well combined. Stir in the vanilla and peanuts.

With the remaining tablespoon of butter, lightly coat two 12-cup muffin tins (each cup should be 2 inches in diameter). Spoon 2 tablespoons of the batter into each muffin cup and bake in the center of the oven for 15 minutes, or until a knife inserted in the center of a brownie comes out clean. Cool the brownies in the pan for 5 minutes, then lift them out with a narrow spatula and transfer to a wire rack to cool.

Short-Crust Pastry

To make one 9-inch pie shell

6 tablespoons unsalted butter, chilled and cut into ¼-inch bits, plus 1 tablespoon butter, softened
2 tablespoons lard, chilled and cut into ¼-inch bits

1½ cups unsifted all-purpose flour
1 tablespoon sugar
¼ teaspoon salt
3 to 4 tablespoons ice water

PASTRY DOUGH: In a large, chilled bowl, combine the butter bits, lard, flour, sugar and salt. With your fingers rub the flour and fat together until they look like flakes of coarse meal. Do not let the mixture become oily.

Pour 3 tablespoons of ice water over the mixture all at once, toss together lightly, and gather the dough into a ball. If the dough crumbles, add up to 1 tablespoon more ice water by drops until the particles adhere.

Dust the pastry dough with a little flour and wrap it in wax paper. Refrigerate for at least 1 hour before using.

PASTRY FOR AN UNFILLED PIE SHELL: To prepare an unfilled, or "blind," pie shell, spread 1 tablespoon of softened butter over the bottom and sides of a 9-inch pie tin with a pastry brush.

Preheat the oven to 400°. On a lightly floured surface, pat the dough into a rough circle about 1 inch thick. Dust a little flour over and under it and roll it out, from the center to within an inch of the far edge of the pastry. Lift the dough and turn it clockwise about 2 inches; roll out again from the center to within an inch or so of the far edge. Repeat—lifting, turning, rolling—until the circle is about ⅛ inch thick and 13 to 14 inches in diameter. If the dough sticks to the board or table, lift it gently with a metal spatula and sprinkle flour under it.

Drape the dough over the rolling pin, lift it up and unroll it slackly over the buttered pie tin. Gently press the dough into the bottom and sides of the tin, being careful not to stretch it. With a pair of scissors, cut off the excess dough from the edges leaving a ½-inch overhang all around the outside rim. Fold the overhang under the outer edges of the dough and crimp it firmly around the rim of the pan with your fingers or the tines of a fork. To prevent the unfilled pastry from buckling as it bakes, spread a sheet of buttered aluminum foil across the tin and press it gently into the pastry shell.

TO MAKE A PARTIALLY BAKED PIE SHELL: Bake on the middle shelf of the oven for 10 minutes, then remove the foil and bake another 2 minutes.

TO MAKE A FULLY BAKED PIE SHELL: Bake the shell on the middle shelf of the oven for 10 minutes, then remove the foil and bake for another 8 minutes, or until the shell begins to brown.

Chocolate-and-Butterscotch Pie

To make one 9-inch pie

3 ounces (3 squares) unsweetened
   chocolate
2 cups light brown sugar
8 tablespoons (1 quarter-pound
   stick) unsalted butter, softened
3 eggs

1 teaspoon vanilla extract
½ cup light cream
A 9-inch short-crust pastry shell,
   partially baked and cooled
   (opposite)
1 cup heavy cream, chilled
1 tablespoon confectioners' sugar

Surprisingly, the uniformly colored filling for this pie will separate as it bakes into chocolate and butterscotch layers.

Preheat the oven to 350°. Melt 2 ounces of the chocolate in a small heavy saucepan over moderate heat, stirring frequently to prevent it from coming to a boil. Set aside to cool to room temperature.

In a deep bowl, cream the sugar and butter together by beating and mashing them against the sides of the bowl with the back of a large spoon until the mixture is light and fluffy. Beat in the eggs one at a time and, when they are thoroughly incorporated, stir in the vanilla, light cream and melted chocolate. Pour the filling into the pastry shell and bake in the center of the oven for 45 to 50 minutes, or until the filling has set. Cool the pie to room temperature.

With a wire whisk or a rotary or electric beater, beat the heavy cream in a large chilled bowl until it begins to thicken. Sprinkle with the confectioners' sugar and continue to beat until the cream forms soft peaks on the beater when it is lifted from the bowl. With a rubber spatula, spread the whipped cream on the surface of the cooled pie, swirling the top attractively. Using the tear-shaped side of a four-sided grater, grate the remaining ounce of chocolate directly over the whipped cream, and serve the pie at once.

Black Bottom Pie

To make one 9-inch pie

CRUST

24 ginger snaps, pulverized in a
   blender or wrapped in a towel
   and finely crushed with a rolling
   pin (about 1⅓ cups)
4 tablespoons butter, melted

Preheat the oven to 375°. To prepare the crust, combine the pulverized gingersnaps and melted butter in a 9-inch pie tin and stir until all the crumbs are moistened. Spread the crumb mixture in the bottom of the tin. Place another 9-inch pie tin over the crumbs and press it down firmly to spread the crust mixture evenly in the bottom and sides of the first tin. Remove the second tin and smooth the top edges of the crust with your fingers. Bake in the middle of the oven for 8 to 10 minutes, or until the crust is delicately colored. Set aside and cool to room temperature.

CUSTARD

¼ cup cold water
1 tablespoon unflavored gelatin
1¾ cups milk
4 egg yolks
½ cup sugar
1 tablespoon cornstarch
A pinch of salt

Meanwhile, prepare the custard and chocolate layer in the following fashion: Pour the cold water into a small heatproof bowl and sprinkle the gelatin over it. When the gelatin has softened for 2 or 3 minutes, set the bowl in a skillet of simmering water and, stirring constantly, cook over low heat until the gelatin dissolves completely. Remove the skillet from the heat, but leave the bowl in the water to keep the gelatin fluid.

In a heavy 2- to 3-quart saucepan, heat the milk until small bubbles begin to form around the edges of the pan. Remove from the heat and cover to keep warm. With a wire whisk or a rotary or electric beater, beat the egg yolks, ½ cup of sugar, cornstarch and a pinch of salt for 3 to 4 minutes, or until the yolks thicken slightly. Beating constantly, pour in the hot milk in a thin stream, then pour the mixture into the saucepan.

Place the pan over low heat and, stirring constantly and deeply with a wooden spoon, simmer for 10 to 12 minutes, or until the custard is thick enough to coat the spoon lightly. Do not allow the mixture to come anywhere near the boiling point or it may curdle. Remove the pan from the heat and stir in the dissolved gelatin.

CHOCOLATE LAYER
3 one-ounce squares semisweet
   chocolate
1 teaspoon vanilla extract

Melt the 3 ounces of chopped chocolate in a small heavy pan set over low heat, stirring constantly to prevent the chocolate from scorching. Measure 1 cup of the custard into a small bowl and set the rest aside in the pan. Stirring the custard in the bowl constantly, slowly pour in the melted chocolate and, when it is completely incorporated, add the vanilla. Pour the chocolate-layer mixture into the cooled pie shell, spreading it and smoothing the top with a rubber spatula. Refrigerate for at least 1 hour, or until the chocolate layer is firm to the touch.

RUM LAYER
4 egg whites   ⅓ cup sugar
⅛ teaspoon cream of tartar   1 tablespoon rum

Then prepare and add the rum layer: With a wire whisk or a rotary or electric beater, beat the egg whites and cream of tartar together until they begin to thicken. Sprinkle ⅓ cup of sugar over the top and continue to beat until the whites are stiff enough to form unwavering peaks on the beater when it is lifted out of the bowl. With a rubber spatula, stir the rum and 2 or 3 tablespoonfuls of the egg whites into the reserved custard. Scoop the remaining egg whites over the custard and, with the spatula, fold them together gently but thoroughly. Pour the mixture gently into the pie, and smooth the top with the spatula. Refrigerate for at least 2 hours, or until the top layer is firm to the touch.

TOPPING
1 cup heavy cream, chilled
2 tablespoons confectioners' sugar
¼ ounce semisweet chocolate

Just before serving, prepare the topping. In a chilled bowl, whip the heavy cream with a wire whisk or a rotary or electric beater until firm enough to stand in unwavering peaks on the beater when it is lifted from the bowl. Beat in the confectioners' sugar, then spread over the top of the pie with a rubber spatula. Using the finest side of a hand-grater, grate the remaining chocolate evenly over the cream. Serve at once.

Key Lime Pie

Originally Key lime pie was made with a pastry crust—and traditional cooks insist it should still be. (For this version, use the fully baked short-crust pastry pie shell described on page 122.) Inasmuch as the pie is at its best when refrigerated and served very cold, a graham-cracker crust—which survives chilling nicely—has been popular, even in Key West, since the mid-19th Century.

To make one 9-inch pie

CRUST
6 ounces graham crackers, pulverized in a blender or wrapped in a towel and finely crushed with a rolling pin (¾ cup)
6 tablespoons unsalted butter, melted

Combine the graham-cracker crumbs and the melted butter in a 9-inch pie tin and rub them between your fingers until the crumbs are evenly moistened. Spread the crumbs loosely, place a second 9-inch pie tin on top and press down firmly to distribute the crumbs evenly over the bottom and sides of the lower tin. Remove the second pan and, with your fingers, smooth the top edges of the crust. Refrigerate until ready to fill.

PIE
6 egg yolks
Two 14-ounce cans sweetened condensed milk
1 cup strained fresh Key lime juice, or substitute other fresh lime juice
1 cup heavy cream, chilled

In a deep bowl, beat the egg yolks with a wire whisk or a rotary or electric beater for 4 or 5 minutes, or until they are very thick. Beat in the sweetened condensed milk and the lime juice. Pour the mixture into the pie shell and smooth the top with a rubber spatula. Cover with foil or plastic wrap and refrigerate the pie for at least 4 hours, or until the filling is firm to the touch.

Just before serving, whip the cream with a wire whisk or a rotary or electric beater until it is stiff enough to stand in unwavering peaks on the beater when it is lifted from the bowl. Spread the cream over the pie, smoothing it and creating decorative swirls on the top with a small metal spatula. Serve at once.

Orange Meringue Pie

To make one 9-inch pie

1½ cups evaporated milk
4 egg yolks
¾ cup sugar
2 teaspoons unflavored gelatin
⅓ cup Grand Marnier or other orange-
    flavored liqueur such as
    Cointreau, Triple Sec or Curaçao
2 tablespoons finely grated fresh
    orange peel
4 egg whites
A 9-inch short-crust pastry pie shell,
    fully baked and cooled *(page
    122)*

In a small heavy saucepan, heat the evaporated milk until bubbles begin
to appear around the edges of the pan. Remove from the heat and cover
to keep the milk warm.

In a deep bowl, beat the egg yolks with a wire whisk or rotary or electric beater for about a minute. Slowly add ½ cup of the sugar and the gelatin, and continue beating for 4 to 5 minutes until the mixture is thick
enough to fall back on itself in a slowly dissolving ribbon when the beater is lifted out of the bowl.

Beating constantly, pour in the warm milk in a slow thin stream. Then
pour the custard mixture back into the saucepan and, stirring constantly
with a wooden spoon, cook over low heat for about 5 minutes. Do not let
it come anywhere near a boil or the custard will curdle. When the custard
is thick enough to coat the spoon lightly, remove the pan from the heat
and stir in the orange liqueur and orange peel. Transfer the custard to a
bowl and let it cool to room temperature.

Preheat the oven to 350°. With a wire whisk or a rotary or electric beater, beat the egg whites to a froth. Add the remaining ¼ cup of sugar
and continue to beat until the meringue is stiff enough to stand in unwavering peaks on the beater when it is lifted from the bowl.

Pour the cooled custard into the pie shell and smooth the top with a rubber spatula. Then spread the meringue on top, mounding it slightly in
the center and creating decorative swirls with the spatula. Bake in the
upper third of the oven for about 15 minutes, or until the meringue is
firm and a delicate brown. Cool to room temperature before serving.

Fresh Blueberry Pie

To make one 9-inch pie

2 pints fresh whole blueberries,
  washed and thoroughly drained
  (5 cups)
1 cup sugar
1 cup water
1 teaspoon grated lemon rind
3 tablespoons cornstarch
A 9-inch fully baked pastry shell,
  cooled *(page 122)*
1 cup heavy cream
2 teaspoons confectioners' sugar

In a 1- to 1½-quart enameled or stainless-steel saucepan, combine 1 cup of the blueberries, the sugar, water, lemon rind and cornstarch. Bring to a boil over high heat, then reduce the heat and, stirring almost constantly, cook for 5 to 10 minutes, until the sauce is thick and glossy. Remove from the heat and, with a rubber spatula, transfer the mixture to a small bowl to cool to lukewarm.

Spread the remaining 4 cups of blueberries out in a single layer on paper towels and pat them thoroughly dry with additional towels. Then spoon them into the pastry shell and mound the berries slightly in the center. When the sauce has cooled sufficiently, pour it into the shell.

With a whisk or a rotary or electric beater, whip the heavy cream in a cold mixing bowl until the cream begins to thicken. Then beat in the confectioners' sugar and continue to beat until the cream is stiff enough to form firm peaks on the beater when it is lifted from the bowl. Spoon the whipped cream into a pastry bag fitted with a plain or decorative tip and pipe a border around the edge of the pie. Or spoon the cream over the pie and swirl the top attractively with a spatula. Serve the pie at once.

Sweet-Potato Pie

To make one 9-inch pie

4 medium-sized sweet potatoes,
   peeled and quartered
4 tablespoons butter, softened
¾ cup dark-brown sugar
3 eggs, lightly beaten
⅓ cup light corn syrup
⅓ cup milk
2 teaspoons finely grated fresh
   lemon peel
1 teaspoon vanilla extract
¼ teaspoon ground nutmeg,
   preferably freshly grated
½ teaspoon salt
A 9-inch short crust pastry pie shell,
   fully baked and cooled (*page*
   122)

Preheat the oven to 425°. Drop the quartered sweet potatoes into enough boiling water to immerse them completely and boil briskly, uncovered, until they are tender and show no resistance when they are pierced with the point of a small skewer or knife. Drain off the water, return the pan to low heat and slide it back and forth for a minute or so to dry the potatoes completely.

Rub the sweet potatoes through a fine sieve with the back of a spoon or purée them through a food mill. Set the puréed potatoes aside to cool to room temperature.

In a deep bowl, cream the butter and brown sugar together by beating and mashing them against the sides of the bowl with the back of a wooden spoon until they are light and fluffy. Beat in the cooled puréed sweet potatoes and, when they are completely incorporated, add the eggs one at a time, beating well after each addition. Add the light corn syrup, milk, grated lemon peel, vanilla, grated nutmeg and salt and continue to beat until the filling is smooth.

Pour the sweet-potato filling into the fully baked pie shell, spreading it evenly with a rubber spatula. Bake in the middle of the oven for 10 minutes. Then reduce the oven temperature to 325° and bake the pie for 35 minutes longer, or until a knife inserted in the center comes out clean.

Serve the sweet-potato pie warm or at room temperature.

Lemon Chess Pie

To make one 9-inch pie

5 egg yolks
¾ cup sugar
1 tablespoon cornmeal
1 tablespoon heavy cream

1 tablespoon unsalted butter,
    softened
2 teaspoons grated lemon rind
¼ cup strained fresh lemon juice
A 9-inch short-crust pastry shell,
    unbaked and refrigerated *(page 122)*

Preheat the oven to 350°. In a large mixing bowl, beat the egg yolks and sugar together with a whisk or a rotary or electric beater. When the mixture thickens and clings to the beater, beat in the cornmeal, cream, butter, lemon rind and lemon juice with a wooden spoon. Pour the filling into the pie shell and bake in the center of the oven for 45 minutes, or until the filling has set. Cool to room temperature.

LEMON CHESS TARTLETS: If you prefer, you can make eight individual tartlets rather than one pie. Roll out the dough as described on page 122 and, with a 4½-inch cookie cutter or glass, cut out eight circles. Fit the circles into eight 3½-inch tartlet shells and refrigerate while you make the filling. Double the ingredients given for the filling and prepare as described above. Divide the filling evenly among the shells and bake in the center of the oven for 30 minutes. Cool to room temperature.

Peach Pie

To make one 9-inch pie

8 medium-sized firm ripe peaches
    (about 2 pounds)
½ cup strained fresh lemon juice
¼ cup sugar

2 tablespoons flour
A 9-inch short-crust pastry shell,
    partially baked and cooled *(page
    122)*
½ cup apricot or peach preserves

Preheat the oven to 350°. Drop the peaches, 3 or 4 at a time, into enough boiling water to immerse them completely and boil briskly, uncovered, for 2 to 3 minutes. With a slotted spoon, transfer the peaches to a sieve or colander, and run cold water over them. Peel the peaches with a small sharp knife, halve them, and remove the pits. Then cut each peach half into ¼-inch-thick slices.

In a deep bowl, stir the lemon juice, sugar and flour together to make a smooth, thin paste. Drop in the peaches and turn the slices about with a spoon to coat them evenly. Then transfer the entire contents of the bowl to the cooled pie shell and spread the peach slices evenly.

Bake in the middle of the oven for 45 minutes, or until the peaches are tender but the slices still intact. Remove the pie from the oven. In a small pan, melt the apricot or peach preserves over low heat. Rub the preserves through a fine sieve with the back of a spoon, then with a pastry brush spread the still warm preserves evenly over the top of the pie. Let the pie cool to room temperature before serving.

Buttermilk Pie

To make one 9-inch pie

6 tablespoons unsalted butter, softened	juice
	1 teaspoon grated lemon rind
1½ cups sugar	A 9-inch short-crust pastry shell,
2 egg yolks	partially baked and cooled (page
3 tablespoons flour	122)
1½ cups buttermilk	2 egg whites
2 teaspoons strained fresh lemon	¼ teaspoon ground nutmeg

Preheat the oven to 350°. In a deep bowl, cream the butter and sugar together by beating and mashing them against the sides of the bowl with the back of a large spoon until the mixture is light and fluffy. Beat in the egg yolks one at a time and, when thoroughly incorporated, beat in the flour. Still beating, pour in the buttermilk in a thin stream, then stir in the lemon juice and rind.

In a large mixing bowl, beat the egg whites with a wire whisk or a rotary or electric beater until they are firm enough to stand in stiff peaks on the beater when it is lifted from the bowl. With a rubber spatula, stir a few tablespoons of the egg whites into the batter, then scoop the remaining batter over the whites and fold together gently but thoroughly.

Pour the filling into the pie shell and sprinkle the top evenly with the nutmeg. Bake in the center of the oven for 40 minutes, or until the filling is firm. Cool to room temperature before serving.

Tyler's Pudding Pie

This recipe is said to have been a favorite of Virginia-born John Tyler, the 10th President of the United States, and was served frequently at the White House during his administration.

To make one 9-inch pie

8 tablespoons (1 quarter-pound stick) unsalted butter, softened
½ cup sugar
1 cup light brown sugar
3 eggs
½ cup heavy cream
½ teaspoon vanilla extract
A 9-inch short-crust pastry shell, partially baked and cooled *(page 122)*
½ teaspoon cinnamon, combined with ¼ teaspoon nutmeg, preferably freshly grated

Preheat the oven to 350°. In a deep bowl, cream the butter, sugar and light brown sugar together by beating and mashing them against the sides of the bowl with the back of a large spoon until the mixture is light and fluffy. Beat in the eggs, one at a time and, when they are thoroughly incorporated, stir in the heavy cream and vanilla.

Pour the filling into the pastry shell and dust the top evenly with the cinnamon-and-nutmeg mixture. Bake in the center of the oven for about 40 minutes, until the filling has just begun to set (it will still be slightly soft in the middle but will become firm as it cools). Remove from the oven and cool to room temperature.

Bourbon-and-Caramel-Custard Pie

To make one 9-inch pie

1½ cups heavy cream
1½ cups milk
1 cup sugar
5 egg yolks
¼ cup bourbon
1 teaspoon vanilla extract
A 9-inch short-crust pastry shell, partially baked and cooled *(page 122)*
¼ teaspoon nutmeg, preferably freshly grated

Preheat the oven to 450°. In a heavy 1- to 1½-quart saucepan, warm the cream and milk over moderate heat, stirring occasionally, until small bubbles appear around the edges of the pan. Cover the pan and set aside off the heat.

Caramelize the sugar in a small heavy saucepan by stirring it over moderate heat until it melts and turns a light golden brown. Stirring the sugar constantly with a wooden spoon, pour in the warm cream-and-milk mixture in a thin stream. Continue to stir until the caramel has thoroughly dissolved. Set aside off the heat.

With a whisk or a rotary or electric beater, beat the egg yolks in a large mixing bowl until they are well blended, then, stirring constantly, slowly pour in the caramel-and-cream mixture, the bourbon and the vanilla extract. Strain the mixture through a fine sieve directly into the baked, cooled pie shell. Sprinkle the top evenly with nutmeg and place the pie in the center of the oven. Lower the heat at once to 350°, and bake the pie about 30 minutes, until the filling is about to set. (The filling may appear somewhat undercooked, but it will become firm as it cools.) Remove the pie from the oven and let it cool to room temperature.

Pecan Pie

To make one 9-inch pie

4 eggs
2 cups dark corn syrup
2 tablespoons butter, melted and
    cooled
1 teaspoon vanilla extract
A 9-inch short-crust pastry shell,
    partially baked and cooled *(page
    122)*
1½ cups pecan halves (about 6
    ounces)

Preheat the oven to 400°. With a wire whisk or a rotary or electric beater, beat the eggs in a mixing bowl for about 30 seconds, or until they are smooth. Beating constantly, pour in the syrup in a slow, thin stream. Then add the cooled melted butter and the vanilla and continue to beat until all the ingredients are well blended.

Pour the egg-and-syrup mixture into the pie shell and scatter the pecan halves evenly over the top. Bake in the middle of the oven for 35 to 40 minutes, or until the filling is firm to the touch.

Serve the pecan pie warm or at room temperature.

BEVERAGES

Mint Julep

Mint juleps are made many ways and Southerners have countless firmly held opinions about which method is right, or best. Though the classic Kentucky whiskey base is bourbon, Georgians often substitute half cognac and half peach brandy; in Louisiana some bartenders use rum, in Maryland they use rye and in Virginia they sometimes add a little cognac to the bourbon. The oldest recipes do not suggest bruising the mint, and you may keep the leaves intact if you do not want the julep to have a pronounced flavor of mint. The following recipe is one version of the classic Kentucky-style mint julep.

To make 1 drink

6 small fresh mint leaves plus 1 sprig fresh mint
1½ teaspoons confectioners' or
superfine sugar
1 tablespoon cold water
Shaved or finely crushed ice
4 ounces Kentucky bourbon

Place the mint leaves, sugar and water in an 8-ounce highball glass or, more traditionally, a silver mint-julep mug. With a bar muddler, crush the mint, then stir until the sugar dissolves. Pack the glass tightly almost to the top with shaved or crushed ice and pour in the bourbon. With a long-handled bar spoon, use a chopping motion to mix the ice and whiskey together. Dry the outside of the glass or mug and chill the julep in the refrigerator for at least 1 hour or in the freezer for about 30 minutes, until the outside of the glass or mug is covered with frost.

To serve, remove the mint julep from the refrigerator with paper napkins or towels, taking care not to wipe off the frost. Garnish the drink by planting the sprig of mint in the ice. Insert a straw and serve at once.

Blackberry Cordial
To make about 1 quart

3 quarts (about 4 pounds) fresh
   blackberries
1 cup sugar
1 tablespoon ground nutmeg,
   preferably freshly grated
2 four-inch pieces stick cinnamon,
    1 teaspoon whole allspice and
    1 teaspoon whole cloves, wrapped
   together in cheesecloth and tied
   with a string
1½ cups brandy

Wash the berries in a colander under cold running water, discarding any stems or blemished fruit. Spread the berries on paper towels and pat them completely dry with fresh towels. Set a fine sieve over a large bowl, and add the berries about 1 quart at a time. Mash and rub them through the sieve with the back of a large wooden spoon.

Pour the blackberry juice into a 3- to 4-quart enameled or stainless-steel saucepan. Add the sugar, nutmeg, and the cheesecloth bag of spices. Then bring to a boil over high heat, stirring with a wooden spoon until the sugar dissolves. Cook briskly, uncovered, for 15 minutes, meanwhile skimming off the foam as it rises to the surface. Remove the pan from the heat and set the mixture aside to cool to room temperature.

Discard the cheesecloth bag of spices and strain the blackberry liquid through a fine sieve into a deep bowl. Stir in the brandy and pour the cordial into a 1-quart bottle or jar equipped with a tightly fitting lid.

Set the lid securely in place. Let the blackberry cordial remain undisturbed at room temperature for at least 3 weeks before serving.

Egg Nog

To serve 12

12 egg yolks
½ cup superfine sugar
1 fifth (about 26 ounces) blended
    whiskey or bourbon
1½ cups dark Jamaica rum
2 cups milk
1 quart heavy cream, chilled
12 egg whites
1 tablespoon ground nutmeg

In a deep bowl, beat the egg yolks and sugar together with a wire whisk or a rotary or electric beater until the mixture is thick enough to fall back on itself in a slowly dissolving ribbon when the beater is lifted from the bowl. Then with a wooden spoon, beat in the whiskey, rum and milk. Cover the bowl with foil or plastic wrap and refrigerate the mixture for at least 2 hours or, even better, overnight.

Just before serving the egg nog, whip the cream in a large chilled bowl with a wire whisk or a rotary or electric beater until it is stiff enough to stand in unwavering peaks on the beater when it is lifted from the bowl.

Then beat the egg whites in a separate large bowl with a clean beater. When they are firm enough to stand in peaks on the beater, scoop the whipped cream over the whites and fold gently but thoroughly together with a rubber spatula.

Pour the egg-yolk mixture into a large chilled punch bowl, add the egg-white mixture and, using an over-under cutting motion rather than a stirring one, fold together with the spatula until no trace of white remains. Sprinkle with nutmeg and serve at once from chilled punch cups.

Tea Punch

To make about 5 cups

6 lemons
2 teaspoons green or black tea leaves
2 cups water
1 cup superfine sugar
2 cups (1 pint) dark Jamaica rum
Finely cracked ice

Using a swivel-bladed vegetable parer, remove the peel of the lemons in spiral fashion, being careful not to cut so deeply as to include the bitter white pith. Set the peel aside in a deep bowl. Squeeze as many of the lemons as you need to make 1 cup of strained juice.

Scald the inside of a glass or china teapot with boiling water, drain, then add the tea leaves. Bring 2 cups of water to a rolling boil in a small pan and pour it into the teapot. The leaves should rise to the top of the pot, then sink slowly to the bottom. (If the water is not at a full boil, some leaves will remain on the top and the tea will be flat or bitter.) Let the tea steep covered and undisturbed for about 5 minutes.

Strain the tea over the lemon peel, add the sugar, and stir until it dissolves. Let the tea steep for about 10 minutes, then add the lemon juice and rum. Mix well, and pour into a 1½-quart pitcher. Cool to room temperature and refrigerate until the punch is thoroughly chilled. (If you prepare large quantities of the tea punch in advance, it may be refrigerated, tightly sealed, for several days.)

Just before serving, fill 4 or 6 glasses almost to the brim with the cracked ice, pour in the tea punch, and serve at once.

Chatham Artillery Punch

Chatham Artillery punch is one of the best-known of the English regimental punches, and has long been a favorite in the South.

To make about 1 gallon

2 ounces green or black tea leaves
6 cups cold water
2 cups strained fresh orange juice
½ cup strained fresh lemon juice
1 quart Catawba or white Rhine
    wine
1½ cups dark rum
1½ cups brandy
1½ cups bourbon
1½ cups gin
½ cup light brown sugar
¾ cup maraschino cherries
A block of ice or ice cubes
1 quart champagne, chilled

Place the tea leaves in a 2- to 3-quart enameled or stainless-steel casserole and pour in the 6 cups of cold water. Cover with plastic wrap or foil and set aside for at least 8 hours, or overnight. Then strain the tea through a fine sieve into a 4-quart bowl. Add the orange and lemon juice, white wine, rum, brandy, bourbon, gin, sugar and cherries, and stir until the sugar dissolves. Cover tightly with foil or plastic wrap and set aside for one to two weeks at room temperature.

    Just before serving, place the block of ice in the bowl (ice cubes can be used but they will dilute the drink by melting too quickly) and pour in the cold champagne. Stir briefly with a glass stirring rod or bar spoon and serve at once, in chilled punch cups or wine glasses.

Pendennis Club Champagne Punch

The following recipe has been adapted from a popular Louisville, Kentucky, punch served at Christmas, but it also makes a refreshing summertime drink. If you plan to use it for this purpose, you may supplement or replace the orange sections with 1 to 1½ cups of seasonal fruits such as hulled strawberries or peeled, sliced peaches.

To make about 2 quarts

1 orange, peeled, with all of the
   white outer pith removed, and
   the orange separated into sections
6 maraschino cherries
1 cup strained fresh lemon juice
   (from about 6 medium-sized
   lemons)
1 cup brandy
½ cup maraschino liqueur
½ cup curaçao
A block of ice or ice cubes
1 quart champagne, chilled
1 pint club soda, chilled

Place the fruit of your choice in a large punch bowl, then stir in the cherries, lemon juice, brandy, maraschino liqueur and curaçao. Refrigerate the bowl for at least 1 hour, then remove and add the block of ice. (Ice cubes can be used, but they will dilute the drink by melting too quickly.)

Just before serving, pour in the champagne and club soda. Stir briefly with a glass stirring rod or bar spoon and serve at once in chilled punch cups or wine glasses.

Recipe Index

NOTE: Size, weight and material are specified for pans in the recipes because they affect cooking results. A pan should be just large enough to hold its contents comfortably. Heavy pans heat slowly and cook food at a constant rate. Aluminum and cast iron conduct heat well but may discolor foods that are made with egg yolks, wine, vinegar or lemon. Enamelware is a fairly poor conductor of heat. Many recipes recommend stainless steel or enameled cast iron, which do not have these faults.

INGREDIENTS: Most of the ingredients called for in this book's recipes can be found at any grocery or supermarket. Few recipes include products that are not widely available. Live terrapin and conch are rarely found outside the southern Atlantic Coast, but frozen or canned terrapin meat, and frozen conch meat, often can be ordered through your local fish store. Fresh soft-shell blue crabs are available only in the late spring and summer months along the Atlantic and parts of the Gulf Coast. A small amount of soft-shell crab is available frozen. Stone- or water-ground cornmeal and whole hominy are available through some supermarkets, gourmet shops and health food stores. Two mail-order sources are Byrd Mill Company, P.O. Box 5167, Richmond, Virginia 23220, and Great Valley Mills, Quakertown, Pennsylvania 18951. Smithfield and country-style hams can be ordered through gourmet shops and local butchers.

Fish and Shellfish

Poultry and Game

Meat

Salads

Vegetables and Grains

Sauces and Dressings

Pickles and Preserves

Breads and Biscuits

Desserts and Candies

Cakes and Pies

Beverages

Notes

All photographs by Mark Kauffman except
page 42 by Richard Jeffery.

✗ Printed in U.S.A.